CIVIL WARS

June Jordan

A TOUCHSTONE BOOK
Published by Simon & Schuster
New York London Toronto Sydney Tokyo Singapore

TOUCHSTONE
Rockefeller Center
1230 Avenue of the Americas
New York, NY 10020

First Touchstone Edition 1995

TOUCHSTONE and colophon are registered trademarks
of Simon & Schuster Inc.

Manufactured in the United States of America

1   3   5   7   9   10   8   6   4   2

Library of Congress Cataloging-in-Publication Data
Jordan, June, date.
Civil wars / June Jordan.—1st Touchstone ed.
p.   cm.
"A Touchstone book."
Originally published: Boston : Beacon Press, © 1981. With new introd.
1. United States—Race relations.   2. Afro-Americans—Social
conditions.   3. Afro-Americans—Civil rights.   I. Title.
E185.615.J67   1995
305.896'073—dc20   95-22173 CIP
ISBN 0-684-81404-8

Grateful acknowledgment is made for permission to reprint the following: "The Voice of the Children" and Linda Curry's poem "My Enemy,"
which originally appeared in *Journal of a Living Experiment*, edited and

(permissions continued on p. 189.)

Acknowledgments

Thanks be to MaryAnn Lash, editor-in-chief, whose instinct and enthusiasm surprised me with joy at the onset of this collaboration.

Thanks be to Joanne Wyckoff, my editor, whose resolute care, decency, and painstaking allegiance to the principles of telling the truth have made the difference, repeatedly, between trudging morale and gusto.

Thanks be to Sara Miles, who literally excavated the mass of these materials from my disorderly files, from the disorderly consequences of a faltering faith, and who ceaselessly said, "Write it down; write it up," and who has illuminated all of this work with the intelligence, and with the valor, of her unstinting moral scrutiny.

Thanks be to Christopher David Meyer, my friend, and my son, whose very life is much of the reason why I am trying to win this one.

j. j.
brooklyn, new york
september 7, 1980

For Christopher
and for Sara
With faith

Foreword

All of this started with my uncle. He was a probation officer living with my aunt and her daughter on the third, the top, floor of our Brooklyn brownstone. Even when he washed and polished his car on weekends, my uncle sported a pistol, most of the time, and told amazing, terrific stories about how he did in this or that unfortunate other guy. I adored him and, I'm pretty sure, he liked me well enough; for example, after his tour in World War II, as a second lieutenant stationed mainly in Georgia, what he brought back for me, as a very special present, was a rather lusty, full-grown raccoon.

For a long while during childhood I was relatively small, short, and, in some other ways, a target for bully abuse. In fact, my father was the first regular bully in my life and there were many days when my uncle pounded down the two flights of stairs in our house to grab the chair, or the knife, or whatever, from my father's hands.

But outside intervention has its limits and, consequently, my uncle decided to teach me how to fight for myself. He showed me numerous ways to disarm/disable an assailant. But what he told me is what I best remember: "It's a bully. Probably you can't win. That's why he's picking the fight. But if you go in there, saying to yourself, 'I may not win this one but it's going to cost you; if you hit me you better hope to take me out. Because I'll be going for your life.'—If you go in there like that they'll leave you alone. And remember: it's a bully. It's not about fair. From the start: it's not about fair."

I quickly, and repeatedly, learned that jumping into a show-down breeds, and requires, a decent degree of optimism, or affirmation, if you prefer: The outcome matters less than the jumping into it; once you're on, there's an adrenalin plumping of self-respect that compensates for terror. I learned, in short, that fighting is a whole lot less disagreeable than turning tail or knuckling under. It feels better. Besides, he was right; I lost a lot of fights as a kid in Bedford-Stuyvesant. But nobody fought me twice. They said I was "crazy."

While my uncle was teaching me literal pugilistics, my parents were teaching me the Bible and sending me out for piano lessons, voice lessons, and the like. Early on, the scriptural concept that "in the beginning was the Word and the Word was with God and the Word was God"—the idea that the word could represent and then deliver into reality what the word symbolized—this possibility of language, of writing, seemed to me magical and basic and irresistible. I really do mean "early on": my mother carried me to the Universal Truth Center on 125th Street, every Sunday, before we moved from Manhattan. I must have been two years old, or three, when the distinctive belief of that congregation began to make sense to me: that "by declaring the truth, you create the truth." In other words, if you lost your wallet you declared, "There is no loss in Divine Mind"—and kept looking. Those words, per se, possessed the power to change the facts; the wallet would turn up again.

I loved words and I hated to fight. But if, as a Black girl-child in America, I could not evade the necessity to fight, then, maybe, I could choose my weaponry at least.

It was the week after the Harlem Riot of 1964, a week of lurching around downtown streets like a war-zone refugee (whenever I heard a police or fire engine siren I would literally hit the pavement to flatten myself before the putative level of the flying bullets) that I realized I now was filled with hatred for everything and everyone white. Almost simultaneously it came to me that this condition, if it lasted, would mean I had lost the point: not to resemble my enemies, not to dwarf my world, not to lose my willingness and ability to love.

This was self-interested, to be sure. As Mrs. Fannie Lou

Hamer said, years later, as she stood on her porch in Mississippi, "Ain' no such a thing as I can hate anybody and hope to see God's face."

So, back in 1964, I resolved not to run on hatred but, instead, to use what I loved, words, for the sake of the people I loved. However, beyond my people, I did not know the content of my love: what was I *for?* Nevertheless, the agony of that moment propelled me into a reaching far and away to R. Buckminster Fuller, to whom I proposed a collaborative architectural redesign of Harlem, as my initial, deliberated movement away from the hateful, the divisive.

My first meeting with Bucky lasted several hours, just the two of us, alone. And when we separated, agreed on the collaboration for *Esquire* magazine, I felt safe in my love again. We would think and work together to design a three-dimensional, an enviable, exemplary life situation for Harlem residents who, otherwise, had to outmaneuver New York City's Tactical Police Force, rats, a destructive and compulsory system of education, and so forth, or die.

This was a way, a scale, of looking at things that escaped the sundering paralysis of conflict by concentrating on the point, the purpose of the fight: What kind of schools and what kind of streets and what kind of parks and what kind of privacy and what kind of beauty and what kind of music and what kind of options would make love a reasonable, easy response?

Forward from that evening in Fuller's room, at the St. Regis Hotel, my sometime optimism born of necessity hardened into a faithful confidence carried by dreams: detailed explorations of the alternatives to whatever stultifies and debases our lives.

My life seems to be an increasing revelation of the intimate face of universal struggle. You begin with your family and the kids on the block, and next you open your eyes to what you call your people and that leads you into land reform into Black English into Angola leads you back to your own bed where you lie by yourself, wondering if you deserve to be peaceful, or trusted or desired or left to the freedom of your own unfaltering heart. And the scale shrinks to the size of a skull: your own interior cage.

And then if you're lucky, and I have been lucky, everything comes back to you. And then you know why one of the freedom fighters in the sixties, a young Black woman interviewed shortly after she was beaten up for riding near the front of an interstate bus—you know why she said, "We are all so very happy."

It's because it's on. All of us and me by myself: we're on.

CONTENTS

PART THREE

Introduction

I

Civil Wars begins thirty-one years ago. And tonight I feel the drifting/shifting of all those years: So much has changed! So much remains the same or worse!

In 1964, I believed I was fighting hard in the middle of an enormous argument about America and anybody's right to be here, specific and nondissoluble. I perceived myself to be surrounded and outnumbered by enemies. I accepted media notions of my "minority" status in a "naturally" white America.

I was searching and furious, and the point was to resist. Uninvited, patronized, or ignored, my wish was, nevertheless, to go on record: To stand on the picket line, to march in the demonstration, to speak at the rally, to write and read the poems, to remember not to forget any of the minutes of the meetings of my one life among so many lives, at risk.

Overwhelmed by public displays of hatred and contempt, self-respect became the chimerical prize I wanted to possess as my own, eventual reward.

Meanwhile, the Civil Rights Revolution was taking place, everywhere, and the consequent display of racist hatred stunned me even as its avalanche of horrors mobilized all kinds of "Negroes"—including myself—into a movement for a nailed-down equality of rights.

In short, there was widespread, savage conflagration for the sake of white supremacy, but we met that awful energy with our own organized and persevering mass revolt.

We did not know that we would win.

We knew that we were right.

II

Tonight it is very quiet. Yes, there is plenty of talk about professional football or the lame mechanics of the recent Academy Awards, but beyond that you cannot find uproar, any political uproar, on the progressive side. On St. Patrick's Day, the President's wife wore a green dress. Fewer Americans smoke cigarettes. And it hasn't rained for seventy-two hours. So what? Is anything going on?

It is thirty-one years after I first published *Civil Wars* and an embarrassing number of Blackfolks vote against "affirmative action," "illegal aliens," federal help for the poor, and preventive, rather than punitive, anticrime initiatives. Disturbing numbers of Blackfolks declare their loyalty to a man who repeatedly beat his wife, another man who called for the murder of Malcolm X, and yet another man convicted of raping a young Black woman.

We profess surprise when hate groups opposed to equal rights for gay and lesbian Americans turn around and target African Americans for scapegoat rhetoric and policies.

"Nigger," "dickhead," "bitch," and "ho' " have long replaced "Brother" and "Sister" as ordinary terms of salutation. And intrafamilial dysfunction, and abuse, have become a too frequent public source for our sorrow and our shame.

Few of us fathom the connection between American inertia in the context of genocide abroad and federal inertia in the context of desperate human need here at home.

On campus, we seldom bother to learn a second language or the history and literature of Chicanos or Native Americans or Vietnamese or, for that matter, Arab or Irish or Jewish Americans.

Meanwhile, a ravaging desire for economic/social and legislated white supremacy fuels an uncommonly loud segment of our population and guarantees a declining, miserable quality of life for Blackfolks, Latino Americans, Chicanos, Asian Americans, Native Americans, children, and an extremely polite female majority. In other words, the quest for white male supremacy jeopardizes most of America. And, to a horrifying extent, our common enemies need to do little more than stand aside and watch the rest of us sink into mistaken animosities. In the wake of Oklahoma City, if anybody thinks the lunatic right will draw distinctions among us, "the undesirable," dream on! We must coalesce or give up all hope of safety!

Civil Wars began thirty-one years ago, and I still believe I am fighting hard in the middle of an argument about America and anybody's right to be here. Immigrant bashing and the Republican-led attack on citizen entitlement flagrantly reveal the chasmic deaths of that developing, awesome disagreement. I am convinced that beneath our blundering conflicts as a heterogeneous national population there are two pivotal questions: Whose country is this, anyway? And who or what is "an American"?

Since 1964, race has been redefined by millions and millions of new arrivals who have begged or borrowed their way onto these shores. Black and white formulations have begun to yield, as they must, to demographic facts of a multiplicity of colors, languages, and legacies, brightening our continental landscape, and our horizons. Correspondingly, our definitions of racist convictions and behavior must be re-examined—and expanded as well: Beyond white hatred for people of African descent, the push for white supremacy punishes, and hopes to extirpate, every people that is not "white" and, also, "Christian." Of course, this necessary redefinition identifies most human beings as members of a hatefully composed target population.

That's the down-side. The good news is that we, the undesirable, vastly outnumber what is, in fact, a national and international minority of dangerous, hyperactive true believers.

Since 1964, issues specific to female life have emerged from traditional invisibility and sorry realms of isolated individual pain. Difficult questions about the meaning and the purpose of female identity have surfaced from fearsome areas of our collective consciousness. And a unifying, global awareness may yet ignite into an overdue, a successful, majority crusade for our fully realized, and liberated, human being.

Sexuality has become an openly political battleground. And class considerations increasingly compel our acknowledgment and response, even while Marxist forms of analysis retain very little of their practical and/or theoretical credibility.

As a Black woman living with change and beset by continuing situations of peril, I am the same and I am different, now. For me, winning has become the point. I have known and I have seen too many people dead, absolutely dead and gone, to settle for resistance or struggle: I am working to win.

Thirty-one years ago death did not seem or feel like anything relevant or decisive. But now whenever somebody dies in spirit or in flesh, I have learned to count that as an inconsolable, irreplaceable loss. I am fighting to enlighten and protect my life by joining with my students, my comrades, and my colleagues for the enlightenment and rescue of all sociable and tender qualities of human life everywhere.

Hatred kills people. Cruelty kills people. Greed kills people. Egomania kills people. Stupidity kills people and trees and water supplies and systems of public education.

But I have come to understand that I am not surrounded by enemies. I teach and I write and I walk and I talk among people who want what I want: Good health, safety, a fair chance at happiness, and a growing environment of friends. I am clear about this: Most folks are really okay, not demonic or heartless or closed. But then it's the powerful few—forever on camera/on microphone—the powerful few who forever keep us inaudible and unknown to each other, or else all the while they disseminate scary disinformation.

We have won many wars for self-determination and for justice since 1964. (The miracle of Nelson Mandela should exorcise any tendency toward despair, or cynicism, any of us may harbor.) And here in the United States, for sure, we have gained greater equality and an increase of lawful protection. But most of us do not know or do not remember how it was before we possessed the freedoms we enjoy, and the avenues of re-course from persecution, or systematic disdain, that our fathers and our mothers labored to secure. And so we have allowed these bitterly earned victories to attenuate, or disappear, en-tirely.

We have forgotten about the power and virtue of moral cer-tainty. We no longer evaluate ourselves or others on the basis of "Right" and "Wrong." We have abandoned an activist, moral language, and our enemies on the "Right" have eagerly moved into that vacuum, proclaiming their bigotries, their violence, and their inhumane policy proposals as God-given, while de-fining the rest of us as *"Wrong."* Genetically, racially, linguisti-cally, and sexually: *Wrong.*

And tonight, I wonder when my people first lost our way. Was it twenty-odd years ago, when Marvin Gaye sang, "There's too many of us dying," and asked "What's Goin' On?" and then, when his own father shot and killed him, we did not run outside screaming with grief and revulsion? Was that when we lost our way? Why did we merely whisper and shrug away our shock?

Was this when self-criticism or self-censure became taboo?

Or did we lose our soul when we failed to embrace "The Welfare Queen" and the young convicted felon as our own, most precious responsibility—our own dearest and nearest in-spiration to redouble our fight for advancement and relief?

Or was it when we tolerated and no longer condemned the worsening desuetude of our immediate neighborhoods and schools: When we forgot the strategy and the tactics of commu-nity control?

Or was it when we began to hate each other? Was that when we lost the faith that must undergird revolt?

I am saying that we have lost our way. We have lost our self-respect. And we have given up on love.

I do not know why.

But there is a hideous, neo-Nazi world view loose on the land. And adherents to that hatred aim to subjugate, or exterminate, everything and everybody who is not Christian and white and male and heterosexual.

Tonight, I'd bet that they will not, finally, triumph. But I am certain that the last call will be horribly close.

In this atmosphere, and in this frightening circumstance, coalition—in the broadest possible sense—seems to me an obvious necessity.

Only an intelligent, coalitional movement can defeat today's politics of exclusion. We need to invent, we need to organize, a political community that includes, and entitles, each one of us. (Period. No exceptions.)

I am thinking of a democratic, a secular, version of the concept of grace: Because you believe, you belong among the blessed. In a democracy, because you exist, you justify and you command all the entitlements you need in order to continue to exist: You belong among the blessed: You are "the people!"

But before going forward, we will have to retrace our steps into an earlier attitude, an earlier certainty, about our American human rights. That grounding will make our love/our self-respect/our future days a likely, and a credible, ambition.

Otherwise, there may be no "otherwise" worth living for.

June Jordan
April 27, 1995

ONE WAY
OF BEGINNING
THIS BOOK

In 1960, I was a very young twenty-four-year-old, interracially married, the mother of a two-year-old son, and living in the housing projects in Queens. At the time, interracial marriage was a felony in 43 states, but in the projects, our many neighbors wondered only if my husband and I had secured parental consent for the relationship we were, evidently, carrying on.

In Erik Erikson's *Childhood and Society*, I had read that the first three years of your life are the most important: they determined your capacity to trust, and to love. This capacity hinged, he said, entirely on the mother-child bonding. So my son, Christopher, occupied the absolute center of my days and my mind, throughout this period. It was a fairly consuming schedule of walks, taking him to the park beside the East River so that he could become accustomed to horizon, to the physical sense of perspective, and conversations and observations and reading aloud and jokes and nightly discussions with my husband, Michael: How's he doing? How was I doing? How are we doing? A regular day could be described as Christopher, Christopher and the house, Christopher and Michael, Michael, and then, when Christopher went to bed, my ongoing work, three or four hours a night, my poetry.

My friend Huck, who had dropped out of Barnard a couple of years before I did, came by, all the way from the Bronx where she lived, about once a month. These visits were, invariably, exhausting. Huck was a genius of sorts; incapable of superficial anything. Hence, any discussion or narrative had to be pursued into the early hours of the morning or it would represent shoddy exploration. Huck had this fantasy, for reasons I don't remember anymore, that I should go away on a vacation to an island in Greece. The question was, she said, what kind of an island, a green one, or a white? (The questions of money or dates were never raised because, clearly, there was neither, in the foreseeable future.) To support this ongoing inquiry, Huck would sometimes bring 25 different picture books that I was then enjoined to examine with her. We would spend hours looking at full-page photographs, black and white, of rocks in Greece, the base or the top of a column in Greece, an old woman walking in the shadow of a cypress tree in Greece, and so on. As the consequence of this fantastic visual inundation, and as means of self-defense against my regular inclination to fall asleep while my friend continued her discourse upon light and dark and inertia and momentum, I began to think about what I was seeing, what I was learning to see. It was in this way that I began to think about architecture: There were photographs, sometimes, that were so beautiful, so simply black and white and variously shaded that my son, Christopher, would sit resting against me on my lap, holding down the page while he stared, in silence, apparently very happy.

While I was coming to believe that black and white offered the most sumptuous, sensually pleasing, and accurate colors for vision, by studying these photographs of Greece, America was plunging into a holocaust confrontation based upon racist perception of black everything as evil opposed to white everything as good.

When, at last, my friend Huck's enthusiasm for the green versus white island discussion diminished a bit, I found myself hooked on that way of looking at things: Architecture became an obsession that I satisfied by, once a week, going into Manhattan on the night the Donnell Library stayed open late, to browse among the architectural journals and textbooks in the downstairs art reading room. This was my one evening out, every week: Michael would come home by six o'clock, if humanly possible, and I would then leave him and Christopher to eat the dinner I had already prepared, and rush to the corner bus stop. At the Donnell I lost myself among rooms and doorways and Japanese gardens and Bauhaus chairs and spoons. The picture of a spoon, of an elegant, spare utensil as common in its purpose as a spoon, and as lovely and singular in its form as sculpture, utterly transformed my ideas about the possibilities of design in relation to human existence. If my mother had held such a spoon, if I could have given her such a useful piece of beauty, even once, perhaps everything would have been different for her: she who committed suicide, not so many years later: she who admired but never wore the dress-up overcoat that my cousin and father and I gave to her, and which she "saved" in the closet, until her death. If I could make things as simple, as necessary, and as wonderful as a spoon of Bauhaus design, then I could be sure, in a deep way, of doing some good, of changing, for instance, the kitchen where I grew up, baffled by the archeological layers of aimless, wrong-year calendars, and high-gloss, clashing wall colors, and four cans of paprika and endlessly, dysfunctional clutter/material of no morale, of clear, degenerating morass and mire, of slum, of resignation.

It was in the Donnell Library that I met Buckminster Fuller: photographs of his inventions led me into a biography and then into his own writings: *Nine Chains to the Moon, Education Automation*, and so on. Even more than Corbusier, Fuller's thinking weighed upon my own as a hunch yet to be gambled on the American landscape where, daily, deathly polarization of peoples according to skin gained in horror as white violence escalated against Black life.

By this time, my regular days alternated with other days when my mother came to babysit while I went into "the city"—Manhattan—for reasons of free-lance journalism or to buy a complete set of WBAI tapes about Robert Williams and Monroe, North Carolina, or to run around with Louis Lomax (author of *The Negro Revolt*) and his friend Tom Johnson (then a feature writer at *Newsday*) and, through a conglomeration of specific story ideas, shared anger, special interest, lovers, drinking acquaintances, and accident, I came to know Minister Malcolm (as he was known at the Temple Number Seven in Harlem),

Jimmy Hicks, then editor of the *Amsterdam News*, Leon Lewis at WLIB, Marvin Rich, national community relations director for CORE, Val Coleman of CORE, James Farmer, then head of national CORE, the late Clarence Funnye, head of New York CORE, Jesse Gray, and Floyd McKissick, among others.

Louis drove a maroon Lincoln Continental that was astonishing on the road, or parked beside the projects where I lived. It was big. While I was researching a story and he making numerous stops to shake hands, gossip, spread rumors, and/or deliver one of his riveting, extempore charismatic speeches at a rally, a not unusual day would nearly conclude by his pulling up in front of the Temple Number Seven Restaurant, headquarters for Malcolm X. There, unable to smoke any of his Cuban cigars, and unable to order his well-beloved double Scotch on the rocks, Louis and Minister Malcolm would review the past 24 hours, analyzing events, scheming ahead: being brothers. There was a lot of uproarious laughter at that table, that immaculate, formica-top table with spindly aluminum legs where Minister Malcolm sat, watching the front door. Always urging us, "You should try the bean pie; I know you'll like it," he was devastatingly hilarious, at will, steadily to the point, and gallantly respectful without exception. He was so clean, his hair cut so short, his suit so plain: it was an austerity, a focus of purposive being that compelled your love and loyalty at once. As I sat between them, Louis and Minister Malcolm, I would sometimes slide into shock, temporarily postponing the questions I had prepared for Malcolm X. This was politics on a dealing level, politics of a national scope that would become headlines and history, at any moment; it was to be a history worked out, in part, by conversations at this small, bare table with the large, clean man behind it. We'd laugh and talk and, leaving, Louis would rave about the Black Muslim purity of lifestyle, their abstinence and discipline, even while he turned the Lincoln Continental in the direction of the Palm Café, on 125th Street, saying, "I could really use a drink; couldn't you?"

At about the zenith of my preoccupation with Fuller's ideas on the one hand, my involvement with Harlem on the other, and the ongoing, central concerns of raising my son, keeping the house, fathoming my husband, from whom I would be, shortly, divorced, working at my poetry, fighting with my parents, developing skills as a political journalist, and the overwhelming assault of the daily news, my friend Huck arrived with another brainstorm.

She had landed a job as a gofer on the motion picture *The Cool World* and, convinced that I should write scenarios and, thereby, combine poetry and architecture in a medium accessible to most people, she tried to persuade me to hang out, on location, and watch the making of this movie. It was being filmed in Harlem, my old homeground. Directed by a white woman, Shirley Clarke, and produced by a white man, Frederick Wiseman, the film "starred" Black kids from the streets; it was the only feature film about what it means to be Black in a racist white country from 1954 to 1964 that I can recall.

Because, as much as possible, I did not want to be away from Christopher, I had to give up my nights at the Donnell for "the movies." I went to watch them shooting on location and ended up assistant to the producer, Frederick Wiseman. That's one way of saying it. Another is, I went to watch "the movie" and I found myself in the middle of my own Black and white life.

ONE

1   Testimony (1964)

First there was Harlem and the people of Harlem, my own birthplace. Then there was the novel about Harlem, *The Cool World*, written by Warren Miller, a white man. Then there were the white people, Frederick Wiseman and Shirley Clarke, who elected to produce and direct a film adaptation of the novel. Then there was the all-Black cast, except for the two or three very minor roles of a teacher and policemen. This cast, primarily composed of Black teenagers chosen for their living resemblance to the characters they were asked to portray, embodied a peculiar experiment, of sorts: Could you learn "to play" yourself? Could kids become professional actors who would act themselves, exactly, and on cue?

In fact, there were a few professionals in the cast, among them Carl Lee, Gloria Foster, Clarence Major, and Gary Bolling. But, overwhelmingly, the cast consisted of kids found on the streets of Harlem and then taken back to these same streets, on camera.

I became interested, and then obsessed, to understand what was going on. Why had Miller written this oratorio of a boy doomed by circumstances? What did these boys think about the trickbag of playing themselves? Who were they, one by one? And how did the grownup crew members view the movie: was it a political undertaking or just another gig, or what?

I began to talk with everybody, and to take notes. Quickly I realized I was investigating an abortion: People had come together with all their hope and all their hatred, but they had separated, permanently, at the last. They had shared that hope but hidden away the longing that made the hope dangerous. They had hidden away the hatred that made the hope impossible.

What began as notes toward an article became a written documentary, *Testimony*, a spoken scenario, in which I used cinematic techniques of jump-cuts and juxtaposition to try and disclose the many dimensions of anything anybody said. By centering on the verbatim statements of each person, and by cutting into the interview, repeatedly, with statements made by other people in the film, I hoped to construct something like a complete frame for the reality of *The Cool World*.

As the interview begins, I am talking with Hampton Clanton, the boy who played the young hero, Duke.

Q. Could you be friends with Duke?

A. Duke is like me. I have the habit of staring a lot. Of fantasies . . .

Q. What kind of fantasies?

A. I always have the fantasy I could go to school and learn about philosophy and economics and things like that . . . and then I have the fantasy from when I was small I could be a actor . . .

Fantasy was a new word for Hampton Clanton: something he'd picked up from *The Cool World*. He pronounced the word with three distinct syllables: fan-tuh-see. Philosophy is a difficult word for him.

Q. What's the name of the book you're carrying?

A. (Reading it) *Marine Power Plant Guide*, by W. B. Paterson.

Q. What's school like?

A. Boring.

Q. Where do you go to school?

A. Food and Maritime High School.

Q. What?

A. Food and Maritime High School. I am the only Negro in my class. They like to put the Negro boys in food. (He interrupted himself to laugh with me.) I am in Maritime . . . I want to do something not greasy, you know? My father is chief engineer at the Hotel Manhattan.

I looked at him as I listened to him and I thought he should be running. His weight is pure. He is like a runner from four thousand years ago but running now across the stone.

Q. How large is your family?

A. There are seven children. I have four sisters and two brothers. The youngest is two years old. My mother lost one this year . . . (He added, because of my puzzled expression) My mother lost one, lost a child this year. It was born and everything, but we lost it . . .

Listening to Hamp, listening to his scarce his sorry words, I wanted to hear other words, but the words I would hear later were the words of other people vividly quarreling about him. Much later I would hear in my mind these quarreling lines tangled abruptly after Hamp's statement:

My mother lost one
Lost a child this year
It was born and everything
But we lost it

"He used to dance in the streets." Hamp's father, *Mr. Clanton*, was proud as he remembered.

"We're talking about a particular person, now. He's not just any Negro," exploded *Leroy McLukas*, the still photographer on the crew.

5

"You people get all excited about one boy." *Charlie Wilson*, the brown-skinned social worker, quickly dismissed the subject.

"Hamp: I was very attached to Hamp," smiled *Madeline Anderson*, the Black production assistant.

"You know he's like a 'soft guy.' Then he's a 'hard guy.' I mean he's cool. Like first he say, 'Man be cool.' Then next time he say, 'Goddamit! Be cool!' Duke you know, he means 'It's gone be like I say.' First he one of the guys. That's all. Then outstanding. Then he the man!" says *Van Dyck*, another teenager in the cast, in his confidential low-tones.

"You know the word *sweetheart?* That's what he is, a sweetheart." Casting director, *Carl Lee*, pitched this line perfectly like a hipster-salesman, nevertheless sincere.

"Remember we don't have a Marlon Brando playing Duke. We have a little kid of the streets." Professional actress, *Gloria Foster*, sat laughing as she spoke.

"Hampton's 3rd grade teacher, she said Hampton was very bright and that he could do anything he wants to," *Mr. Clanton* said matter-of-fact.

"Is he mentally deficient? Everything he tries, fails." The light baritone of the Black technician on the set touched on Duke with hostility.

No beginning grew by not
beginning again

birth returned but by raving
later than began
the beginning never again
begun

Shirley Clarke, the director, discussed Hamp and Duke by using their names interchangeably as though they were inextricable identities prey to identical difficulties and meriting the same, warm regard: "Duke? Duke *is* Hampton. I *see* him as Hamp. You can't help loving Hamp. That's why we chose him. Duke is an absolutely criminal case of not having opportunities, etc. He should be a doctor. He has such enormous humanity. I say he *should* be a doctor, but what's going to happen to him? I've been thinking about private school for him. It might work. He's young, isn't he? (Hamp is sixteen years old.) I don't know. But look, he's still going to that dumb-assed school. You better not put that down, edit it or something, but isn't that what it is. It's a dumb-assed school. He needs to go to a school, learn how to think, how to read, how to talk."

Van Dyck: "He's my man—I go over and think he want to shoot some crap. But he say all the time: 'Man, help me with my lines . . . Help me with my lines.' "

Q. Did you feel like reading that book I loaned you? (*Catcher in the Rye*)

A. Yes. I tried to read it, but . . . (Hamp stopped and studied his wrist.)

Q. You didn't think Holden was like Duke?

A. No. See, Duke wants a lot. He wants a gun. He wants to be big. He wanted to go down with a blade like a man, not like a kid, but Holden seem like he don't want anything he have . . . Holden have a lot . . . and Holden wasn't giving a lot of respect for his mother. I didn't think he was like Duke.

Q. What did you think of Duke's feelings for his mother, what were they?

A. Duke was closest to his grandmother.

Van Dyck: "I love my grandmother and she love me."

But he had a lot of respect for his mother. She always hollering at him, but she did love him . . .

Van Dyck: "She smack the shit out of me and that's the way it supposed to be."

I know a lot of white boys who would scream and curse at their mothers, but Duke didn't do this . . .

Q. What about *The Cool World,* is it true what it says?

A. Those boys out in the street, it's the same. They mess with other guys and everything but an adult they don't bother. They say, "yes miss, no miss." I mean Negro boys: for them adults are different.

Q. Is Duke a hero?

A. Duke is not a hero, he's a regular boy, the leader of a gang.

I asked Shirley Clarke, specifically: What about *Duke* in *The Cool World?*

Clarke: "His problem is how to get someone to hear you're alive. If everyone puts you down you know, how are you going to stand up? I mean if someone thinks you're shit —then what are you going to do? You think maybe you are shit. You know, some of these boys do things just to get their names in the paper?"

Q. How come so many kids belong to gangs? You don't, for example.

A. They belong mostly for protection. Most boys rely on themselves, have to rely on themselves . . . Because who can you tell, what you going to say?

Q. Was there any special scene where your own life helped you to perform?

A. The San Francisco scene. I was thinking about how one of my friends who was beaten up by one of the rival gangs had passed away and how it would have been if we had spent our whole lives together . . .

Q. What did you think of the San Francisco scene? (Duke and fourteen-year-old Luanne talk quietly in bed. They have just learned of Littleman's murder. She tells her dream to Duke: To go to San Francisco so that she can see the ocean: She has never seen the ocean.)

A. I wanted to cry
I wanted to really cry
but I was afraid I'd be doing
something wrong.
Something held me back but
I wanted to cry

Fred Wiseman, the producer: "One of the investors said, 'I won't do it. I won't because of that boy, Duke. I don't like the boy playing Duke. His face: he has that same sullen impassive face typical of African impassivity.' What does *that* mean?"

I didn't know; I didn't answer Fred.

Q. Hamp, what was your memory of working for a white female director?

A. It was easier to talk to Carl (Casting director, Carl Lee). Carl was a man and a Negro . . . I want to do the whole film over . . . This time do it right . . .

Q. What friends did you make? Did you make friends with the other boys?

A. I feel easier you know, with boys (Negro) instead of adults (white).

Q. What sort of a working day did you have, was it a hard one?

A. Well, we work nineteen-twenty hours a day. A fourteen-hour day is a "short day."

Q. You must have been exhausted!

A. Next morning I feel like I could hardly make it. But my mother she say, "You got a job, this is work you got to do." And you know I see how this is helpin' them, helpin' the family and everything, and that's how I make it.

Q. What do you think this film will do, will it help?

A. If I would have thought that this would make our race look lower than it is, I wouldn't have done it at all . . .

Q. Did the film resemble your own life?

A. Thurston's apartment is like mine, but you know, higher class.

(Thurston's apartment is in a public housing project—a scene eliminated from the film. Thurston was somebody who had made it out of the projects, to college out of state.)

Q. Are you consciously aware of problems as a Negro in N.Y.C.?

A. I belong to this club meets every Friday. They talk about segregation. I step in there if it's cold.

Q. What techniques of acting did you learn?

A. Well, Carl told me "acting is living."

Q. And you do want to be an actor now?

A. Yes.

Q. Does that mean that now you want to be alive, to live differently?

A. I guess so. Yes ma'am.

Q. What is the difference since working on the film?

A. I like to be like Father Logan. I like to do social work. Help people. I like to go to acting school. You think I could go to a school like that?

Carl Lee explained: "The big problem was the lead kid.
Father Logan called me. He was very interested in one
boy . . . the kid had a terrible record, a really bad record
(but you talk to him and he's the shyest kid!). I went
down and looked at this kid. He had his right-hand man
with him . . . we chose his right-hand man . . . a better
choice we could not have made: Hamp is a very rare
human being . . . there really is this problem of being a
kid (but) almost a man."

Q. If you want to be an actor or a social worker what would
   you have to do?

A. I have to go to night school besides to get an academic
   diploma.

Q. Have you spoken with an adviser at school?

A. Yes. But she don't have time yet to see me I guess. She have
   a lot of boys to take care of.

Q. Does anyone give you guidance counseling at school?

A. No. You have to ask the teachers but they never have the
   time.

Van Dyck: "They's 6,000 students, they don't know
you by your face, they know you by your seat."

Q. Hamp, do you play any musical instrument?

A. Well I like to play the piccolo, because I try to find out
   which one goes the highest. And the piccolo goes the highest. Is that right?

Q. I think so. But have you ever played the piccolo?

A. My family we always talking about it but I never have one
   yet. Like my mother she going to buy a drum for me, say
   Friday, and then Friday come and no drum . . .

11

After coffee, Hamp and I wandered down Broadway in the Times Square district.

Q. How's it going to be when your name is here with all these lights and people in line to see you in the movie? (Hamp stopped where we were and slowly pivoted in order to take in the whole glossy scene.)

A. That be all right. That be pretty nice.

We laughed. The next time I heard from Hamp, he was coming to my home. There was snow in the sky, in front of the faces on the street and on the ground about two feet deep. It was something like a blizzard. Hamp called to check on the directions, and as he was bold enough to ignore the snow, I went to meet him at the subway station.

In twenty minutes only five or six people emerged, cowering from the snow. At last I discerned a figure rising on the stairs. Bareheaded, shoes shined as they sank into the drifts, casual and leisurely in his approach, Hamp surveyed the strange terrain, and then approached the covered car that honked. He was eager to continue the practice of talking ... about himself.

Q. Where were you born?

A. In North Carolina. I came to New York City when I was two. We lived in Harlem on the West Side ... For two years. Harlem is where things began: a lot of heartaches. I used to go with my mother and father to places, like the Apollo. I used to be standing up in chairs and hollering and people would be throwing money, rent money at me ...

Q. What did you think of Shirley Clarke?

A. I think she's unusual. She's not soft like some women. So it was easier to do.

Q. You think a movie about race problems can help Negroes to better themselves?

A. I think it's only harmful if it makes you self-conscious

about being a Negro . . . Did you know Hermit was changed to a Muslim?

Q. No. What do you know about the Muslim Movement?

A. A lot of boys at school talk about Black Muslims. One boy, a Muslim, he telling the teacher off, from what I hear. And he know what he's saying.

Q. What did your father, Mr. Clanton, think of the scenario for *The Cool World*?

A. He thought it was all right. My father always told me not to do what other people do. So I used to be loaning money for future good luck. Like I always used to loan money. I figure it bring me good luck later on. Like it cumulate, add up and I have good luck . . . like that's probably why I got into the picture . . .

Hamp made me wonder what he got out of the picture He has a word. Fantasy is his word for the reasonable expectation of a school to cultivate his mind and train him usefully to enter a labor market that is not rapidly diminishing, as is the market for semiskilled labor.

Given every circumstance providing for paralysis, Hamp had the desire to act. He had the desire to deviate from the turning of the trap; he had the desire to become an actor. And for a half year, his very life was in a cataclysm; reality *required* this desire.

The plot of *The Cool World* reveals a group of Negro boys who, because they are outside the "legitimate" structure of power, construct their own. They have their gang. And because the leader exists without a feasible goal that is as motivating as it is "acceptable," he has his personal obsession; he wants a gun.

Manrique, a psychiatrist/expert on young people: "Death becomes a means of being alive."

But even this is denied him: He never gets his gun.

This history of enforced impotency was embodied by Duke who was embodied by Hamp. This was supposed to be acting

13

or in other words, this history was supposed to be somewhere untrue for Hamp. Thinking that there must be a discoverable distinction between Hamp's life in "the cool world," and Duke's meaning in *The Cool World*, I made this call:

Q. Is this Charlie Wilson?

A. Yes.

Q. And you are a Counselor of Rehabilitation with the Board of Education?

A. That's right.

Q. I've been talking with a boy who has the leading role in a film about life in Harlem. And he needs help.

A. Where does he go to school?

Q. Food and Maritime High School.

A. Oh. That's the dumping ground for "I.Q.'s" of *80*. A little bit above and quite a bit below.

Q. This boy wasn't dumped there. He *chose* to go there so that he could be trained for a definite job. He was ill-advised.

A. Well what would you guess his "I.Q." is?

Q. About *160*.

A. *(Screaming)*: Listen! You mustn't become emotional about this. Don't get too emotionally involved!

Q. I'm not being emotional, Mr. Wilson. He's handicapped, but he could have an I.Q. of about *160*.

A. *I* don't know anybody with an "I.Q." that high!

Q. I'm sorry. But what can be done to get this boy out of that "dumping ground" and into a school?

A. What does he want to do?

Q. He'd like to learn how to read . . .

Hamp: "I'd like to learn how to read, for myself, a book like *An Actor Speaks*, that somebody gave me, or *Negroes With Guns*, that somebody else gave me, you know?"

A. He'd have to be what you call an individual referral—they'd sit him down and try to straighten him out: Rehabilitate him.

Q. That's what I'm telling you. He doesn't need straightening. He's great as he is. He needs development—preservation, not rehabilitation.

A. *You see you people get all excited about one boy. There's nine thousand of them and here you are worrying about just one.*

Q. I couldn't very well call you up about nine thousand boys, could I, Mr. Wilson? You're a Negro, Mr. Wilson. Don't you know how it is a Black boy can be absolutely isolated from guidance and without an example?

A. Sure I know. And I know there's nothing you can do for those people. It's the fault of the parents—

Q. But Mr. Wilson, never mind . . .

I was too busy driving the car to look at *Dorothy Oshlag*, associate producer, when she said, "Harlem is more important than any one of its people."

Later, talking with Malcolm X I asked him:

Q. Did anyone in the film particularly impress you?

A. I was very impressed by the gang leader, what's his name?

Q. Duke. His real name is Hampton Clanton.

A. Hampton Clanton. You should bring him around to see me. I'd like to talk to him.

Minister Malcolm smiled at me.

2 Letter to Michael (1964)

Finally, the film was born, in 1964. That had been my goal: to get the film out, to see through birth some version of the truth of this Black and white experiment. We were all exhausted. But that felt fine: At least we had tried hard to show something real about Black life in this country. After the premiere at Cinema 2, I could barely keep awake for the short trip home to the projects, across the 59th Street Bridge.

I remember that night: I was very drunk and my friend, Tom Johnson, was pretty well along, himself. We listened to Billie Holiday for a while. And then he left. You can't really celebrate a waste. Even if you put the thing on film, that's what it is: a film about the death of another Black boy.

My husband was away at the University of Chicago, finishing up his graduate studies in anthropology. Or so I thought. In the meantime, I had undertaken full support of the family. Michael was in Chicago but he could have been on Mars. Working on the film and living in the city in the spring of 1964 engulfed me, totally, in upNorth variations of the racist storm convulsing America.

I left the film company that spring and began my career as a free-lance journalist. My first commission, based on an editor's reading of *Testimony*, was a piece for the *Herald Tribune* on the Freedom National Bank at 125th Street, a bank owned by Black people and serving the Black community. After that, Clay Felker at the *Tribune* asked me to determine whether or not there would be "a long hot summer" in Harlem. My investigations led me to the conclusion that there would have to be/that there *should* be a long hot summer because, as I titled my essay, "nothing is new for the man uptown."

Felker refused to accept my findings. He had, he told me, a very good Negro friend who had reassured him that there just wasn't any kind of Negro anger around that even resembled the rage I had sought to articulate. Felker left to cover the Republican convention in California that would nominate Goldwater. He said we'd finish the argument when he returned.

I'd had some notion that if the reasons for rage could be known, then the powers that be would move to eliminate them. But, anyway, Felker left. That weekend was the weekend of the Harlem Riot of 1964. My ace running buddy during the riot was Bostic Van Felton, one of the boys from the cast of *The Cool World*. I wrote to Michael about that night.

... I lay in bed that Sunday, reading, sleeping, and lazy. Close to dinnertime, I suspected the heat had somewhat abated and chose to walk almost as far as the bridge in order to gain the benefits of such exercise and in order to buy the N.Y. *Times*. As I dressed, I turned on the radio. Newscasters seemingly competed in hysterical warnings and reports of official pleas to the Harlem community not to duplicate the preceding night's terror. This was the first I knew of the Saturday night riot. I disbelieved, as a matter of principle, the hysteria and took off on my hour's walk. Returning from the distant drug store, I scanned the paper and learned that funeral services for fifteen-year-old Jimmy Powell would occur that night. I had been shocked and enraged to read two or three days earlier of the murder of this boy, half the size of the big, Irish cop wearing no uniform and electing to shoot a kid who allegedly held a pen knife. This cop, Gilligan, is the recipient of citation for four times disarming men. I decided to pay my respects to the boy.

Angry little Dorothy Moscou came by, shared my dinner and accompanied me to the funeral establishment. Once we were off the Triboro Bridge, we had entered a challenge to credulity.

Literally scores and scores of helmeted, white policemen patrolled the streets in hubs of 25 or 30 each. Harlem was extremely quiet. There were more policemen than people on any main street. We parked. Dorothy was now nervously joking about going home. I offered to drive her back, but she refused the offer. I went to the Theresa Hotel to look for the CORE people in that office. There was a crayon-printed sign on the closed door indicating that the office had moved west on 125th St. I went down the hallway to the Muslim Mosque and found it dark and empty. Dorothy Moscou and I threaded our way through the sidewalk mushrooms of police. We were heading for the funeral of the boy. The presence of so many policemen began to make me nervous, frightened, and angry. We went to the 38th parallel: 132nd St. and 7th Avenue. Past this corner, no one was allowed. Buses began to arrive, taxis, civilian automobiles, fire engines with sadistic screeching—all vehicles jammed with policemen. The territory was clearly invaded. I could not believe it when still another bus would brake to a stop at that intersection and disgorge still another hundred combatants. Overhead, helicopters dawdled and dived and contributed to the unreal scene of a full-scale war with no one but enemies in view. After a while, my corner was filled by about a hundred people standing and talking among themselves: "WHAT THEY DOING HERE?" "WHY THEY SO MANY POLICEMEN?" "THEY AIN LETTIN NOBODY THROUGH DERE." "SHITMAN. I LIVE ON THAT STREET. WHAT AM I SUPPOSED TO DO NOW?"
"COP KILLED A KID."
"YEAH?"
"MAN, WHERE YOU BEEN YOU AIN HEARD FIFTEEN-YEAR-OLD KID GOING TO SCHOOL: WHITE COP SHOOT HIM JUST LIKE THAT."
"THEY'S KILLED MY SON. THEY'S KILLED ONE OF OUR CHILDREN."
"SO WHAT THEY DOING HERE?"
It was approaching that time when the parents of young Powell were expected to drive from the funeral home. Tension was so great, anger at the bewildering multiplication of cops, guns in

hand, helmets on their heads, snarling expressions on their faces, was mounting and suddenly I decided I was in danger. I ran across the street to an outside phone booth. Cops shouted at me. I kept running. Got inside the booth and called Huck. Told her where my car was and asked her to call Lillian for money if I needed either medical attention or bail. The crazy thing was the way, suddenly, I could feel implacable danger. In the middle of a sentence I hung up saying: OH SHIT. Bullets were flying past the booth and all about me. I doubled over and raced in doubled-over fashion, down 7th Avenue. I was ready to vomit from fear. When the noise of the firing stopped, I edged back to the same corner. I was angry now. So was everyone else. I wanted to know what the hell had provoked the deadly barrage. Women had begun to stand and scream, simply scream and not move. I looked for Dorothy. I couldn't find her. I was afraid she'd been wounded and raced back to my car but could not find her. I returned to 132nd St. and 7th Avenue. A group of kids, mostly boys thirteen and fourteen years old, were slowly swaying up 7th Avenue: WE WANT MALCOLM X WE WANT MALCOLM X   WE WANT MALCOLM X. The cops, one of them blew a whistle, those immediately behind him began shooting into the air as they ran to crash into the kids, the cops behind the first group dropped to the street on their knees and bellies and took aim and fired and fired and fired. Men and women around me were screaming and running in an hysterical fashion. A man with conked hair took his bottle of cheap whiskey from his pocket and hurled it through an auto appliance store window, smashing it. Reporters hurdled the center island of the avenue and, hiding behind the cops who were taking aim, began to shoot their flash bulbs. TV crews careened into the mess with more police arriving every minute, fire engines wildly swinging into the hive of vehicles, sirens screaming although there was, of course, no traffic. What was left of the boys linked arms: WE WANT MALCOLM X   WE WANT MALCOLM X . . . These kids were desperate now, tears coming down their cheeks. The TV crews quickly set up and as the boys and the front line of cops neared each other, there were the TV strobe lights illuminating the confrontation. It was a nasty, bizarre circus, and nauseating. Behind me there was now more shooting. Cops ran from the corner of 131st St. and 7th Avenue, shooting up into the air yelling at us to go home, while from the corner of 132nd St. an identical huddle of shooting cops ordered the same thing. It reminded me of dodge ball. I couldn't get off the block. Nobody could. We were trapped and terrified.

Bottles began to pelt the street aiming at police cars, policemen. Every time there was a hit, the probably thousand of us on both sides of that street would yell and applaud. Cops were firing endlessly now. They would stand on the curb and fire up at all of the windows of the tenement buildings. People were screaming obscenities MOTHER FUCKERS SHITS WHITE SHITS WHITE MOTHER FUCKERS BASTARDS MURDERERS GILLIGAN GILLIGAN.

I was sweating so much now from fear and from running back and forth that my dress, red ordinarily, was simply very dark. My hair was flat on my head with sweat like water streaming on my glasses making it difficult for me to see. Multitudes of teenagers began arriving from the projects opposite where we were trapped and throwing anything they could find and taunting and being wounded. I was backed up against a laundromat store window with about fifteen other people. A young boy and girl, at the most fifteen, stood obvious on the sidewalk, she crying uncontrollably, he holding her close to him and becoming a man in this hideous night for her sake. All of us watched this, silently. A girl next to me pushed her boyfriend: WHY DON'T YOU GO OVER THERE AND HELP THEM? He said: WHY DON'T YOU? They were teasing each other. She pushed him, playfully, forward. He pushed her back. She pushed him. He pushed her, she pushed me, I fell back on someone else and the window behind us caved in. Instantly we were the duck targets for the cops who concentrated their fire on us. I began running and knocking people over. Someone grabbed me by the arm: JUNIE JUNIE. It was Bostic. I hugged him. He made room for me in his doorway. A young man with a CORE armband came by begging everyone to stay next to the store windows, away from the sidewalk. I asked him what was going on at CORE headquarters. He told me it had been converted into a first aid

20

station. Bostic and I determined to get there however long it would take. We did. It was jammed. People were cursing and drunk and bleeding and phones were ringing. Bostic and I were assigned to go and get James Farmer who was supposedly at 131st St. and 7th Avenue, and bring him back to talk to the Governor who'd just been contacted. We charged out wondering how we would get past the cops. Got in my car, got as far as 130th and 8th Avenue. There a cop told me to pull over and began abusing me. I nudged Bostic who opened his door and split. It took me an hour to return to the office. Once there, I shook Farmer's hand, watched Bayard Rustin fail to dent the chaos and finally leave. I began helping a white doctor, Douglas Hitchings, who turned out to be a psychiatrist. He was a volunteer, the only medical volunteer we had. He refused to leave even though all whites were ordered to accept escort out of the area. He and Bostic and I began running out to answer street emergency calls from teams scouting Harlem making 15 minute reports. Police were using grenades and machine guns. You needed a CORE ID card to get past any corner. My main accomplishment that night was not to vomit. I had never seen the back of a bashed-in head, a kneecap split by a bullet—blood. Hitchings returned to the office. I took over the phone. Writing down reports. Then Bostic and I went over to Harlem Hospital. People sat on waiting benches, blood pouring from wherever they'd been hit. Attendants literally mopping and mopping up the blood and guts on the floor. All was quiet at Sydenham Hospital: they would not accept any emergency patients after 1 A.M. We were trying to get together master lists of wounded to give to Val Coleman down at the legal office. This was to prove a permanently impossible goal. Such horrifying chaos. Farmer would return to CORE headquarters every hour or so after going to one of the two police precincts in order to ascertain the number of arrests, the charges, the physical condition of the arrested. He looked like a large, dead man. We all felt completely defeated. Only the endless harassment of danger, of really running from the guns, kept all of us awake and going.

At about 2:30 A.M., I took a look at Bostic. He's absurdly loyal to me. He looked about to pass out, so tired was he. I had

21

no money to buy anything for us to eat or drink, even if any stores had been open. They'd all been closed at 7 P.M. on Sunday, in any case. I told him to go home. He said he wouldn't go home until I did. So I had no choice but to drop him at his house shortly after three. The next morning, or that morning, he was to be at work at nine. What a kid. What was terrible was the devastating effect on Bostic—the sight of Negro men and women at the CORE headquarters eating each other up, shouting and fighting and swearing rather than sanely getting together against the outside enemies. I made it over the 59th Street Bridge and drove to the candy store at Queens Plaza and bought the *Herald Tribune*.

The rest you know. Except that the N.Y. *Times, Life,* and the local TV teams who put together specials attempting to fathom the riots, were commendable, I think, in not duplicating the *Tribune*, the *News*, etc.

Monday night was more of the same but less. I picketed Rockefeller's town house at 62nd St. and 5th Avenue on Tuesday night. Passers-by would call us commies, disgusting. The police were provocative and hostile. GILLIGAN? MUST GO!

Good for the soul. I could barely move Tuesday night when I got home.

. . . So I guess that's that. This is long, but I took you at your word that you wanted some kind of mangled account. If I failed to write it in—these were events of HORROR auguring no good whatever. Every seventh word, by the way, in the Harlem crowds, was GOLDWATER. My sentiments exactly.

3 Letter to R. Buckminster Fuller (1964)

A week after the riot, my husband wrote, saying he was not coming back.

Another week went by. *Esquire* asked me to write for them. I proposed a collaboration with Bucky Fuller; he was the only person I was willing to try; maybe working with him could save me from the hatred I felt, and the complete misery I felt, the want.

When it became firm that Bucky and I would collaborate on an architectural redesign of Harlem, I put my whole life on the line: Now I would work and work and work and wait on this beginning, as a writer, thinker, poet.

There was no money. The advance, gallantly extracted from *Esquire* by Bucky, went quickly. Christopher could not come back to me from his grandparents because I had no money to support him. Michael was gone. I worked. I studied architecture. I wrote to Bucky. I planned. I spent my life waiting. It was a gamble.

Those days I didn't eat. A few friends brought me cigarettes, Scotch, eggs, bread, and my mother gave me two or three dollars for gas money. What I had left was my car: my tangible liberty was my car. I lived like this until *Esquire* said, okay, you're done: It will be published. That was seven months away.

That December, Bucky came to town. We met. I showed him my final draft. He approved it. We walked over to *Esquire*. They approved it. They said they'd send me the money. It came: December 24, 1964. Christopher came back: December

24, 1964. I pleaded with the bank to cash the check, immediately. I went to the airport and recovered my son. On our way home, we kept stopping to buy food, a Christmas tree, presents for Christopher, presents for friends who would come by, and that Christmas Eve I was a millionaire in love, spending 500 dollars before the doors were locked for the night.

In our plan for the redesign of Harlem, Fuller addressed himself to a main worry of mine: Too often, urban renewal meant Negro removal, as the street saying phrased it. Serious improvement of a physical community where Black people lived almost always meant the literal eviction of Black families while redevelopment took place and then exclusion of these families by means of subsequently high rents they could not afford.

When I told Fuller that most of the tenement structures in Harlem were only six stories high, he came through with a brainstorm whereby you would build the new dwellings above the old: the first floor of the new housing would correspond approximately to the seventh floor of the old. During construction of the new housing, Harlem residents would therefore be able to continue living in the old housing directly underneath. Then, once the new structures stood completed and in place, the old would be razed, entirely, and Harlem families would literally move up into their new homes. The enormous ground area freed by the demolition of the tenements would now be converted into communal open space for recreation, parking, and so forth.

Our design would achieve economies of cost per unit as the result of scale: providing for the total redevelopment of a community of 250,000, the design justified "tooling up" a mass manufacturing facility capable of producing the necessary number of units. This project, we thought, would have enormous, national, showcase impact, besides. It would demonstrate the rational feasibility of beautiful and low-cost shelter integral to a comprehensively conceived new community for human beings.

We conceived of this environmental redesign as a form of federal reparations to the ravaged peoples of Harlem. We fully expected its enactment. In this spirit, we worried over every problem and detail related to maximal speed, practicality, and economy.

When the article appeared in the April 1965 issue of *Esquire*, with the results of our collaboration ascribed entirely to Fuller, the editors referred to it as "an utopian plan." These same editors called the piece "Instant Slum Clearance." My title had been "Skyrise for Harlem."

This is a letter I sent to Bucky, early on.

Dear Mr. Fuller,

I hope you are very well. The following four pages represent my effort to organize our undertaking into an outline ... My feeling is that the text should *complement* the visual presentation of our proposal and not simply explain/duplicate the visual presentation of our design. The limitation of 2500 words seems to me arbitrary and acceptable only if it becomes possible to adequately condense to a poetry of form the verbal aspects of the piece. Please advise me of your reaction.

Recently I was able to get away to the country for several days. As the plane tilted into the hills of Laconia, New Hampshire, I could see no one, but there was no tangible obstacle to the imagining of how this land, these contours of growth and rise and seasonal definition could nurture and extend human life. There was no obvious site that might be cleared for housing. No particular grove nor patch visually loomed as more habitable, more humanly yielding than another. And yet, I surmised no menace of elements inimical to life in that topography. It seemed that any stretch, that every slope, provided living possibilities. With just a tent and a few matches, just the minimum of provisions could convert a randomly selected green space into human shelter. Perhaps one explanation of this easy confidence is that such land clearly suggests the activities required for construction of efficient shelter and, further, these requirements imply necessary labor both feasible and quickly rewarding for human beings to accomplish.

25

By contrast, any view of Harlem will likely indicate the presence of human life—people whose surroundings suggest that survival is a mysterious and even pointless phenomenon. On the streets of Harlem, sources of sustenance are difficult to discover and, indeed, sources of power for control and change *are* remote. Nor is labor available—labor that directly affects, in manifold ways, the manners of existence. Keeping warm is a matter of locating the absentee landlord rather than an independent expedition to gather wood for a fire. This relates to our design for participation by Harlem residents in the birth of their new reality. I would think that this new reality of Harlem should immediately reassure its residents that control of the quality of survival is possible and that every life is valuable. Hospital zones where strict control is exercised over noise, dirt, and traffic serve as examples of peculiar exception to city habits of chaotic indifference to environmental functions on behalf of human life. I am much heartened by your insistence on the invention of a physical device rather than efforts of social reform. I also believe that the architecture of experience deeply determines an incalculable number and variety of habits—i.e., the nature of quotidian existence.

. . . The map you kindly gave me indicates Mt. Morris Park and Morningside Park in Harlem. Mt. Morris Park *is* just a rock. Morningside Park does not function as a pleasurable means of escape from entirely man-made environments. These two might well be replaced by park-playgrounds such as I have seen designed in the studio of your friend, Isamu Noguchi.

I plan to explore the New Jersey coastline just below the George Washington Bridge to see if another bridge might be justified between New Jersey and New York at a level invading Harlem. From the Lincoln Tunnel to the George Washington Bridge is quite a leap. Similarly, might there be a possible unification through design of the convergencies of the 8th Ave. Subway, the IRT Subway, and the N.Y. Central Railroad on 125th Street?

I notice on the map that, from W. 125th St. to W. 155th St., the land body of Manhattan is progressively squeezed as the Harlem/East River swerves westward. And, as you see, the sense of green space as a center of island life ends once you stand north of W. 110th St., with the termination of Central Park. While Riverside Drive affords some park area to the west of Harlem, there is no corresponding usage of the eastern shore. Now, this last year, N.Y.C.'s Planning Commissioner, William F. R. Ballard, has attempted to proceed toward two aims original with his tenure of office. One is the construction of waterfront housing and the use of waterways for daily transit. His second aim is the procurement of a feasible, master plan for New York City. Apparently, N.Y.C. has had nothing that even resembles a master plan since 1811!

I wonder if our plan for Harlem could provide for access to shoreline and thus to natural fluency that would devolve from dwelling places alternating with circles of outdoor safety along the water's edge. This would mean domestication of the littoral, but not the occlusion of the autonomous energies of the river. Would you think it worthwhile to connect interior green space with peripheral rivers?

And interconnection—an arterial system of green spaces leading to water; an arterial system psychologically operative from any position in Harlem. For example, a concentric design with the perimeter touching water east and west. Interior orbitry would spot open spaces—plazas, playgrounds, campus, parks.

Given our goal of a pacific, life-expanding design for a human community, we might revise street patterning so that the present patterns of confrontation by parallel lines would never be repeated. The existing monotony limits pleasures of perspectives. Rigidly flat land is ruled by rectilinear form. The crisscrossing pattern too often becomes a psychological crucifixion; an emergence from an alleyway into a danger zone vulnerable to enemies approaching in at least two directions that converge at the target who is the pedestrian poised on a corner.

I suppose I am appealing for as many curvilinear features of street patterning as possible. This bias seeks to overcome physical patterns of inevitability; the sense of inexorable routes, the impossibility of differentiated approach, of surprise. All of these undesirable effects now result from the gridiron layout of city blocks.

I remember the comparison you drew between the two professions of architecture and medicine. If the physician had continued healing practices determined by the criteria of tradition and expectation, his practice might well have lost its justification, namely, the patient.

I would wish us to indicate the determining relationship between architectonic reality and physical well-being. I hope that we may implicitly instruct the reader in the comprehensive impact of every Where, of any *place*. This requires development of an idea or theory of place in terms of human being; of space designed as the volumetric expression of successful existence between earth and sky; of space cherishing as it amplifies the experience of being alive, the capability of endless beginnings, and the entrusted liberty of motion; of particular space inexorably connected to multiple spatialities, a particular space that is open-receptive and communicant yet sheltering particular life.

4 The Voice of the Children (1967)

In 1967, Herb Kohl, one of the founders of Teachers and Writers Collaborative[1] asked me to join the program. For myself, this meant an unorthodox entry into unorthodox teaching. The idea was that of enablement: The encouragement of Black children to trust and then to express their own response to things. The poet/writer collaborated with a public school teacher in the construction of a workshop to which the teacher would invite kids that he or she knew might be interested or, at least, curious. After each workshop session, the poet was required to write a diary account of the proceedings and send same to T & W headquarters, then located at Teachers College, Columbia University.

While many poets/writers went to work within an actual classroom, I began my workshop on Saturday mornings, in East Harlem. My partner was Terri Bush, a young white woman from Biloxi, Mississippi; it was her husband, Dr. Jim Bush, who tried to save the little girl victims of the racist bombing of the Sixteenth Street Church in Birmingham, Alabama, 1973.

Terri and I continued our collaboration even through a transfer of the workshop to Brooklyn. Eventually, we found a regular home in the basement of a church in Fort Greene, Brooklyn. Our workshop for Black and Puerto Rican teenagers grew into

[1] For more on Herbert Kohl, see his book, *36 Children* (New York: New American Library, 1973). A full account of Teachers and Writers, including my own participation, can be found in the book *Journal of a Living Experiment*, edited and with a commentary by Philip Lopate (New York: Teachers & Writers Collaborative, 1979).

the central point of reference in our lives, and in the lives of the children we came to know as intimately as members of a family. My son, Christopher, somewhat resignedly agreed to wake up early, each Saturday, so that we could drive from our Bronx apartment down to the Church of the Open Door, in Brooklyn. He and I joined the kids, and Terri, on the weekly expeditions that followed the workshop: trips to Prospect Park, museums, Jones Beach, and to the Chock Full O' Nuts near Columbia which we picketed because the guys there refused to serve our group when we made a high-spirited entry, one particular afternoon.

By 1970, the kids had reached a state of happy renown so that colleges and radio stations frequently asked them to give poetry readings. This was fabulous confirmation for these young people and, in turn, they gave the audience everything they had, which was a whole lot, indeed.

Terri and I compiled a representative sampling of their prose and poetry. Titled *The Voice of the Children*, this anthology was published by Holt, Rinehart and Winston in 1970.

On March 23, 1973, one of these children, one of the most beautiful children ever born into this world, Michaelangelo Thompson, died. He was murdered by the Cumberland Hospital in Fort Greene: They refused to treat him when he arrived on a stretcher, bleeding from the head. Michael's father pleaded with the hospital staff in the emergency room to help Michael, to save Michael, but it was too late. Finally, an ambulance came from another hospital, hours after Michael had sustained the fractured skull. Michael reached the second hospital dead on arrival. Michaelangelo Thompson was thirteen years old.

These are some of my diary writings from the Teachers & Writers Program, as well as a letter to Zelda, T & W's director, about a young Black writer, Deborah Burkett.

———————

October 7, 1967

It was cold and an almost early morning time when anyone coming, they thought, to teach somebody else how to write, or to write with other people at their elbows, had to walk in one of three or four ways up and down streets in order to reach the Community Resource Center.

You could walk along 116th Street where, toward noontime, there would be a lot of people with very little money, altogether, ransacking cardboard boxes for two-dollar dresses and socks, six pairs for one dollar. One hundred sixteenth Street is where you can't find a bathroom if you need one. It is not similar to Macy's. And the movie houses on that street always offer you a choice of rubraw garbage that depends on monsters for entertainment. Entertainment here is taken as distraction: If you distract families who live in completely pre-occupying boredom/crises, then you have entertained them. So there are monsters, and then there are horror stories, and then there are varieties of "the incredible"—offered to families who know that unbelievable things are hopelessly routine.

I approached the Center from 2nd Avenue, walking west on 117th Street and I felt cold, but I saw one beautiful brick building that rose from the broken sidewalk squares to a low height I could easily hold within my comfortable eyes, and the bricks were separate one from another and the coldness of the morning was steady freeze into the separation of the bits and pieces that come together and eventually mean disintegration of shelter and of heat, which is to say, the falling apart of possibilities of survival that is worth writing about. Or living. I am not sure, any longer, that there is a difference between writing and living. And I thought, maybe I will say that to the kids and maybe that is how we will begin writing together, this morning.

October 21, 1967

This day's workshop continued for a bit more than an hour and a half, and it would have easily continued longer except that I had obligations elsewhere, as well. During the time we were together many things happened, indeed, so many moving things happened that I wished, that I wish I could simply talk it into a tape rather than scrunch the experience onto paper.

First, I would like to say I do not know what I can offer the kids who come on Saturday. Except for two of them (sisters), the others come with a shocking history of no education in language. That they come ought to shame all the so-called teachers who have perpetuated this history of no education. But shame will not help these young people. And my question is, what will be helpful?

I had to control my sense of desperation. I wanted to say, wait a minute. Let's stop right here. This is a Sentence. This is Not a Sentence. *Him* is spelled with an *m*, not with an *n*. Words that sound alike, or a little like each other are Not spelled the same way. For instance, *along* is not the spelling for *alone*, and *dried* is not the spelling for *died*.

Then I thought, if this total lack of preparation characterizes the English "education" of these kids, then editors and personnel managers are just going to have to take the consequences. And/or portable tape recorders will have to replace the ballpoint pen. But, horribly, this is absurd. *The kids* are going to take the consequences of all the shit treatment and despisal-pedagogy imposed on them. So, I repeat, what should I try and do? How should any of us try to alter the probable consequences—on Saturdays, yet?

For further instance of the meaning of the question I am raising: Now there are two weeks of writing on paper. It is obvious to me that one thing to do is to have them typed up and, eventually, made into folios that each kid can keep. But apart from making something they have done seem more permanent and seem more valuable via a kind of simple-minded, physical change of appearance, what should I do? Should I "correct" them? How can you correct completely illiterate work without entering that hideous history they have had to survive as still another person who says: You can't do it. You don't know. You are unable. You are ignorant.

So, for the moment, I am not doing that. And the question is what *am* I doing?

We sat about the large table and I set out paperback copies

of Gwendolyn Brooks' poetry and poetry by Langston Hughes and *Modern Poetry in Africa.* I said, "Why don't you look over these books and then we'll talk about them, or we'll write about something in them, and you can keep whatever you like—if you like them." Some of the kids looked at me to see if I was kidding. The hesitation was so real, I finally handed around copies.

Pat Curry (thirteen years old) and her sister Linda (fourteen) ventured: "We wrote these things. You want to see them?" Pat had written a composition called "My Theory of Lies." Linda had written a poem called "Who Am I." Both of these things are worth reading, indicate talent, and were furthermore voluntarily undertaken—and accomplished on their Friday lunch hour.

Then everybody started reading. In the extreme quiet, Marion B. gave me a story David had written, called "The Big Bear." He has even illustrated it. It's a good story, very carefully crafted and written down in a fastidious, painstaking way. I started to say something to him. David was holding on to the Brooks poetry book for dear life. I waited until he began to turn a page. Your story is beautiful. He really smiled.

Around the table a fantastic thing was happening. One would show another a particular poem—secretively, with extreme delight, nervously, giggling, furtive—as though they could not really believe what they were reading. As though they were reading "dirty books" and might be caught. The furtive sharing grew into a very animated kind of interaction. Finally I asked Linda if she'd had any books like these in school. She looked at me to see if I was putting her on. "No," she said. "We don't have any book! They give us *Scope.*"

"*Scope?*" I asked. "What's that?" Marion B. volunteered: "It's a paper the schools distribute. Like a scholastic magazine."

"You mean," I asked Linda again, "you mean you don't have any poetry, any stories. Any books like that?"

"No," she said, managing her surprise at my ignorance, politely.

Then I suggested that if anybody wanted to read any poem she liked, or he liked, aloud, they should just do so.

Well, it got to be like the most beautiful kind of neo-Quaker meeting: There would be this extreme silence, and then somebody would just start reading aloud a poem. Victor read a poem. Thayer Campbell read a poem. Everybody except me read a poem, or two or three poems. Some read aloud embarrassed, or defiant, or giggling, or quiet. Others, like Deborah, who last week said she couldn't write about power because she always loses everything, Deborah who is ridiculed by the others as stupid, so slow, etc., *Deborah* said, "I want to read one." We all stared in surprise and waited. She read "Freedom" by Langston Hughes. Later she read "Christ in Alabama." David sat next to me fantastically intense in his meticulous copying of a poem by Gwendolyn Brooks: "The Chicago Defender Sends a Man to Little Rock." I said to him, "You can keep that book, you know?" He shook his head. "I know," he answered. David wanted to copy it down. First he copied the opening five-line stanza. Then, firmly, he declared, "I want to read one." And he read what he'd copied. Then he copied two more lines. And later read them. Finally he read three more lines he'd copied. In more than an hour and a half, David had copied, in an indescribably devout manner, ten lines of poetry. What will you do for next week, David? Without the slightest pause he answered, "I'm going to write poems. And bring some I wrote already."

December 9, 1967

Following the conclusions of last week's report, Christopher and I came to the Resource Center equipped with a phonograph, copies of fables produced through the Teachers & Writers Collaborative, photographs likewise produced, paper, pencils, and these record albums (long-playing): Dinah Washington, Billie Holiday, Little Walter, and Johnny Griffin. My intention was to introduce the kids to Little Walter, who makes latter-day rock groups look silly and sound trite, to introduce them to the completely different, roots-originating styles of Washington and

34

Holiday, and to try to interest them in jazz via the Griffin group.

We were going to write songs. Nobody was there. Nobody came.

Victor Cruz and I sat talking, dispiritedly. We both felt demoralized. Victor said this was the last day, anyhow. I was stunned to consider this might be so.

"What do you think was accomplished?" I asked him.

"The experience of failure."

"But is that worth having?"

"Oh yes, it's very valuable."

So we were gloomy with value.

"They didn't like this place," I said. "They thought it looked like a slum."

"It does," says Victor.

"No books," I remarked.

"No continuity," says Victor.

Instead of the kids coming all the way from Brooklyn, we, or I should have gone there. It's too far. It's too much on a Saturday. It's too little: only Saturday.

"For an hour," Victor added. "These people have problems, plus then you start telling them times and places, they can't make it. Should be where the people are. Get to know them. They get to know you. Come when they can."

Should be down on a first floor. And local.

Victor and I fell quiet. He would soon be moving into East Harlem and have a pad on the premises of a local workshop. If things worked out.

I would not be moving to a place more convenient for the kids. When I said "the kids" I had faces in my mind, and names and a difficult accumulation of memories geared always to Next Time. There would be no Next Time, now. What had happened, then? I wanted to throw the phonograph out the windows on the third floor, the windows that could not be opened. But I wanted it to be playing as it went down. And I wanted The Kids to watch it go and hear it crazy in the air and all of us dancing where it would land. Tough. The ashtrays were clean on the table and I left the empty room empty.

TRAVEL

I would like to go
Where the golden apples grow

Where the sunshine reaches out
Touching children miles about

Where the rainbow is clear in the sky
And passersby stop as they pass by

Where the red flamingos fly
Diving for fish before their eyes

And when all these places I shall see
I will return home back to thee

The end

by Deborah Burkett

February 12, 1968

Dear Zelda:

Enclosed please find a copy of the children's writings from last week. They are my report on our Saturday Workshop. Here, I wish to answer your letter of the 9th.

Deborah's poem, as you acknowledge, differs from Stevenson's. You say hers is superior. I say hers is her own poem. I submit that Deborah's not only equals the arresting force and loveliness of Stevenson's, it makes a very different statement—as any proper reading and comparison of both poems would reveal.

Contrary to your suggestion, Stevenson was not "foisted" on Deborah. In my opinion, Deborah is a clearly gifted writer. And she has presumed, she has dared to do what other clearly gifted children do: They learn by a kind of creative mimicry. They consume and they incorporate, they experiment, and they master. Perhaps your letter derives from the fact that this particular gifted child is Black and poor. Black children who are poor (or, one might extend it to Black children poor or not) are supposed to learn nothing in school and life from the streets. That statement's awful accuracy depends upon the facts that teachers of Black children do not, generally, teach, and that the street, or that being alive, per se, provides inescapable instruction.

Evidently, Deborah is an exception. And, there are exceptional children who are Black. Deborah has been learning the streets and she has been learning in school and in the library. Rather than question her demonstrated learning, one should feel relief. Would you have her know only what she fears and what threatens her existence?

Contrary to your remarks, a poet does not write poetry according to the way she talks. Poetry is a distinctively precise and exacting use of words—whether the poet is Langston Hughes, or Bobby Burns.

One should take care to discover racist ideas that are perhaps less obvious than others. For example, one might ask: Will I accept that a Black child can write "creatively" and "honestly" and yet *not* write about incest, filth, violence, and degradations of every sort? Back of the assumption, and there is an assumption, that an honest and creative piece of writing by a Black child will be ungrammatical, misspelled, and lurid titillation for his white teacher, is another idea: That Black people are only the products of racist, white America and that, therefore, we can be and we can express only what racist white America has forced us to experience, namely: mutilation, despisal, ignorance, and horror.

Fortunately, however, we have somehow survived. We have somehow and sometimes survived the systematic degradation of America. And therefore there really are Black children who dream, and who love, and who undertake to master such "white" things as poetry. There really are Black children who are *children* as well as victims. And one had better be pretty damned careful about what one will "accept" from these children as their own—

their own honest expression of their dreams, their love, and their always human reality that not even America can conquer.

According to your letter, one might as well exclude nineteenth-, eighteenth-, seventeenth-, and sixteenth-century literature from the libraries frequented by ghetto students. For, inasmuch as they are young, inasmuch as they are children, *they will learn*, and they will assimilate and, happily, they will master.

Do you suppose that ghetto schools should merely extend the environment that has murdered millions of Black children? The inculcation of self-respect and healthy race identity does not follow from the mere ventilation and reinforcement of deprivation in every one of its hideous forms.

No great poet has emerged without knowledge and mimicry of precedent. Even William Blake is no exception to this generality. And yes there *are* Black children who will insist on becoming great writers who are Black the way Shakespeare was an Englishman.

I think Deborah may be one of these children. I hope so. And I will continue to try to serve the kids who come on Saturdays, one at a time, as this child and that child—rather than as Black children wholly predictable and comprehensible in the light of statistical commonplace.

5 On Listening: A Good Way to Hear (1967)

In 1967, the *Nation* published this essay; the editors changed the title to "Spokesman for the Blacks."

If you want to know how somebody feels or thinks, ask him. If he can't tell you in words you understand, ask someone else. Not anybody else, but someone else. A relative of the man. A close friend. Somebody who seems to you very similar. And when you resort to these sources of information, qualify the value of your data: call it secondhand or worse.

This may strike you as elementary. And yet, there is a man who exists as one of the most popular *objects* of leadership, legislation, and quasi-literature in the history of all men. There lives a man who is spoken for, imagined, feared, criticized, pitied, misrepresented, fought against, reviled, *and loved*, primarily on the basis of secondhand information, or much worse.

This man, that object of attention, attack, and vast activity, cannot make himself be heard, let alone be understood. *He has never been listened to.* He has almost never been asked: What do you want? What do you think? Coverage of a man scream-ing in crisis is not the way to hear him think.

That man is Black and alive in white America where the media of communication do not allow the delivery of his own voice, his own desires, his own rage. In fact, the definitely preferred form of communication, Black to white, is *through* a white intermediary—be he sociologist or William Styron. This is true. I know it, and, nevertheless, I have been amazed by the phenomenon of Nat Turner *alias* William Styron. Or is it: the alien phenomenon of Nat Turner *via* William Styron?

Since this publishing event amounts to some kind of climax, it may be worthwhile to review the reviews: One, in the *New York Times*, was titled "The Slave Who Became a Man." Translation: The slave (the object) became a man: He spoke in the first person. *He spoke as subject*—courtesy of William Styron, of course. Still, there is progress: a Black man speaking as subject—albeit an imaginary speech coming from the imagination of a white man.

And how does the white intermediary regard his rôle? (*New York Times*, 10/8/67) Styron: "It was a challenge . . ." met on the basis of . . . "rank intuition." Very good.

How do other white men regard the intermediary?

> I think that only a white Southern writer could have brought it off . . . A Negro writer, *because of a very complex anxiety* . . . would have probably stacked the cards, producing in a mood of unnerving rage and indignation, a melodrama of saints and sinners.—*New York Review of Books, October 26, 1967 [Italics mine.]*

Having read and reread the above, I have a question for Philip Rahv, whose opinion it represents: Are you kidding?

If not, then let me make plain that you would have to reject *The Confessions of Nat Turner, by Turner*. Mickey Rooney can write his memoirs, Gertrude Stein can write the "autobiography" of Alice B. Toklas, but you're not having any "confession" by Nat Turner, unless it's an outright fake.

The few facts on Turner, a religious "saints and sinners" fanatic, illuminate your view. First, he was a Black man: not somebody you hear. Secondly, he was a slave, an object: objects don't talk. Third, he took off one night, with as many other Black men as he could find, to murder white Southerners who kept him in slavery. He went, a man full of fury and avenging spirit, to find flesh and bloody objects of his wrath: to find white men who had never been able to understand that he was not "a slave," *not an object* on which to quietly rest their contempt. His account would have been pretty damned one-sided. And, no doubt, his mood was that of "unnerving rage and indignation."

Instead, indeed, we have "a white Southern writer" who has "brought it off." But Styron's stunt merely gives point to a season of fantastic, Black-to-white "dialog" miscarried by white-controlled media through the "medium" of the now professional, white intermediary.

This has been the season when (white) Ross Wetzsteon reviewed (white) Shane Stevens' book about Black people living in Harlem. Stevens' novel, *Go Down Dead*, lumps along in the fashionable first-person-by-rank-intuition, and bears a strangely close resemblance to an older, white author's novel about Harlem, Warren Miller's *The Cool World*. You could even say that Stevens comes across like a poor copy. On the book jacket of *Go Down Dead*, one finds John Howard Griffin, *white* author of *Black Like Me* (sic) declaring, "It is authentic." Grotesque arrogance is somebody like Griffin judging the "authenticity" of white fiction about Black life. Nor is the complete circus, the virtual incest of white reviews of white books about Black life, amusing.

As a matter of fact, Stevens' "authenticity" is taken for granted by Wetzsteon, in *The Voice*. There, the reader learns that, once and for all, the myth of rhythmic, graceful Negro speech has been exploded. On the contrary, I submit that, once and for all, the demerits of presumption have been clarified: Warren Miller's Duke Custis spoke his mind and his dreams in some of the most beautiful and rhythmic sentences ever printed. Miller happened to have been a writer gifted with an extraordinary, accurate, and willing ear. Shane Stevens is something else. And I should not have to worry about Stevens, his deficiencies or aptitude. I should not have to hope, I should not have to care about the multiplying, white interpretations of me, of Black people. We should have an equal chance to express ourselves directly.

Back in the real world, this is the season when (white) Jerry Tallmer reported James Baldwin's return to America. Tallmer "quoted" Baldwin's definition of Black Power: "It means the self-determination of evils" (New York *Post*, 8/25/67). That particular Black man, Baldwin, never said anything of the kind. He said, "It means the self-determination of a nation of people." (The ear was willing, but the hearing poor?)

This is the season when Houghton Mifflin released (white) Jonathan Kozol's *Death at an Early Age: The Destruction of the Hearts and Minds of Negro Children in the Boston Public Schools.* In an interview, Kozol observed, "There's nothing in my book that Negroes couldn't tell you themselves." Exactly. As regards ghetto public "education," there's nothing in his book that Negroes have not been *trying* to tell. That's what the busing was all about: an attempt, by Black parents, to dilute the consistency of an "education" serving to lower I.Q. scores and reading levels of Black children. And that's what community school boards are now about, in lieu of the bus, and in view of the manifest impossibility of "integration." The bitter history of I.S. 201 is a case in point. But the spirit and the pace of Kozol's testimony is, altogether, that of a white man; a free man; a stranger to destructive, overpowering circumstance: the ghetto. His testimony, for these reasons, is new, and may succeed where expressed weariness of suffering has failed.

Malcolm X spent a determining part of his life in that same Roxbury section of Boston where Jonathan Kozol, in the words of one reviewer, underwent "radicalization" as a fourth-grade teacher, for eight months. In a completely other sense, and by his own account, Malcolm X also underwent "radicalization," in Roxbury. And afterward, Malcolm X repeatedly condemned the *systematic* "destruction of the hearts and minds of Negro children" in the public schools of Boston, Milwaukee, Chicago, Charleston, Los Angeles, Houston, New York, etc., etc. (Was anybody, anybody white, listening to him?) Jonathan Kozol is not Malcolm X. But Kozol is honest. "Radical" or not, he is rare. To judge by contemporary vogue, he could as easily have written, and published, a sensational book entitled "Last Year at Gibson: I Was a Fourth Grade Negro Student." But Kozol is honest; he tries to be honest.

Death at an Early Age documents the fact that some members of the libertarian, enlightened, white minority—very very very very slowly—realize something is hideously wrong. Put differently: the virulent, demonstrated racism of the white majority can—*itself*—eventually nauseate and outrage otherwise retiring, timid, and "innocent" (oblivious) young men like Mr. Kozol. I would like to ask him: What took you so long? *Seven months* before you reacted, before your hand was pushed to the paper that might expose an obvious horror. But I am being unfair, perhaps, and irrelevant. The point worth noting is that Kozol came to the ghetto, saw what was happening there, and changed his understanding *on the basis of firsthand experience.*

Further, he minutely recorded the daily methods whereby Black children learn that they cannot be taught, and that, in any case, there is nothing they will be taught about themselves and their heritage that will help them survive, much less inspire them to self-respect and great achievement. And in so recording the days of his awakening, Kozol describes the terrible fragility of courage and, by implication, the immense need of it—among whites.

Kozol's *Death* is really about segregation: about the vicious consequences of differing people being forcibly separated—by tradition, fantasy, employment, unemployment, and reasons of hatred. At best, segregation only precludes the commitment of a Jonathan Kozol—*before* he went to the Gibson School in Roxbury. More commonly, American segregation produces white "teachers" who continue to obviate the potentiality of Black children in ghetto schools.

Death at an Early Age is happily free from rhetoric. It should open a powerful, public debate. It should already have done so. E.g., this being the case, what are the possibilities for change?

After reading it, I mistakenly assumed that half the reviews would be solicited from Black adults who remember waiting at their schoolroom desks for somebody to recognize them, *as students.* Or that reviews would be solicited from among Black community leaders of local school boards. But not at all. To my knowledge, and to the knowledge of Kozol's publisher, every single review has been white. From the variety of their backgrounds (some of the "critics" never went to public school, never taught children, and so forth), it would seem that the main qualification was *status as an intermediary*. No relative, no close friend, no adult who was once one of the "Negro children," *the objects* of sympathetic, horrified description, has been asked: What did you think then? What do you think now?

I will not forget my conversation with a "liberal" literary editor:

I: "Who's reviewing Kozol's book for you?"

He: "———"

I: "Is he white?"

He: (surprised by the question) "Yes. Why?"

I: "It's unfortunate, given the subject matter, that there won't be a Black review anywhere."

He: "Oh. But the reader won't know the difference."

Let me tell you: there is a difference. There is a difference Black from white in this country. And the reader, the general public is not going to know the human meaning of that difference as long as *dialog-by-intermediary* rules the press and the rest of it. The white problem will never be solved as long as American Black life is an imagining, a TV spectacular, the product of rank intuition, the casualty of gross misrepresentation, and grist for statistical games. The white problem will never be solved as long as American Black life remains an object, a titillation, a scare, an unknown reality, and an unfamiliar voice. Black people have been speaking as subjects, as first persons, as the only persons we are—for longer than it took to "radicalize" Jonathan Kozol. Is anyone, is anyone white, preparing to listen?

6 Black Studies: Bringing Back the Person (1969)

In the fall of 1967, Herb Kohl called me at home, very late one night. He was supposed to begin teaching at City College the next morning and he had decided that was impossible: He needed to write, full-time. Would I, he asked me, take the job instead?

I was sure Herb was kidding. I had never taught anywhere, had no college degree, and what in the hell would I be teaching, anyway?

"Freshman comp," he answered me, calmly. "What's that?" I wondered. But Herb is pretty persuasive and, at the last, after he promised to check with the Chairman of the English Department, and then let me know the outcome of their conference, I agreed to take the class.

The Chairman said he would be very pleased if I'd join the faculty so I spent the night crash-rummaging among my books in order to choose a course curriculum reading list. The next day we began, the freshmen and I, with Whitehead's *Aims of Education*.

In this way I began my teaching career on a university level. At the time, the English faculty of City College included these poets and writers and thinkers: Toni Cade Bambara, Addison Gayle, Jr., Ray Patterson, Barbara Christian, David Henderson, Adrienne Rich, Audre Lorde, and Mina Shaughnessy. Toni Cade Bambara walked with me to my first class. "Are you nervous?" she asked. I laughed, nervously. "Anything you have to give, just give it to them," she said. "They'll be grateful for it."

All of these people were soon to become much more than colleagues. City College was split between faculty and Third World students who wanted to inaugurate an Open Admissions policy, on one side, and faculty and students who viewed the Open Admissions concept as an intrinsic atrocity which, if implemented, would catapult the University into a trough of mediocrity, at best. Those opposed to Open Admissions argued, in effect, that the people, as in a democratic state, preclude excellence: excellence of standards and of achievement.

In every sense, from faculty petitions to student manifestoes, to the atmosphere in the cafeteria and the bathrooms, City College signified a revolution in progress. Nobody was eating, sleeping, thinking, or moving around anything except the issues at stake.

When the Third World Students raised the red and green and black nationalist flag on the campus flagpole and closed the campus until our demands were met, we opened what we called A Free University at Harlem's I.S. 201. It was exhilarating: we were furious and fighting. And we won.

I wrote this essay, published in the *Evergreen Review*, October 1969. It is, if you will, a position paper.

———————

All my life I had been looking for something, and everywhere I turned someone tried to tell me what it was. I accepted their answers too, though they were often in contradiction and even self-contradictory. I was naive. I was looking for myself and asking everyone except myself questions which I, and only I, could answer.
                                    —*from* Invisible Man *by Ralph Ellison*

Body and soul, Black America reveals the extreme questions of contemporary life, questions of freedom and identity: *How can I be who I am?*

We lead the world stubbornly down the road to Damascus knowing, as we do, that this time we must name our god. This time, gods will grow from the graveyard and the groin of our experience. There will be no skyborne imagery, no holy labels slapped around our wrists. Now we arise, alert, determining, and new among ourselves. I am no longer alone. We move into community of moment. We will choose. But not as we were chosen, weighed and measured, pinched, bent backwards, under heel. Not as we were named: by forced dispersal of the seed, by burial of history, by crippling individuality that led the rulers into crimes of dollar blood.

We, we know the individuality that isolates the man from other men, the either/or, the lonely-one that leads the flesh to clothing, jewelry, and land, the solitude of sight that separates the people from the people, flesh from flesh, that jams material between the spirit and the spirit. We have suffered witness to these pitiful, and murdering, masquerade extensions of the self.

Instead, we choose a real, a living enlargement of our only life. We choose community: Black America, in white. Here we began like objects chosen by the blind. And it is here that we see fit to continue—as subjects of human community. We will to bring back the person, alive and sacrosanct; we mean to rescue the person from the amorality of time and science.

History prepares the poor, the victims of unnecessary injustice, to spit at tradition, to blow up the laboratories, to despise all knowledge recklessly loosened from the celebration of all human life. And still, it lies there, the university campus, frequently green, and signifying power: power to the people who feed their egos on the grass, inside the gates.

Black American history prepares Black students to seize possibilities of power even while they tremble about purpose. *Efficiency, competence:* Black students know the deadly, neutral definition of these words. There seldom has been a more efficient system for profiteering, through human debasement, than the plantations, of a while ago. Today, the whole world sits, as quietly scared as it can sit, afraid that, tomorrow, America may direct its efficiency and competence toward another forest for defoliation, or clean-cut laser-beam extermination.

Black American history prepares Black people to believe that true history is hidden and destroyed, or that history results from a logical bundling of lies that mutilate and kill. We have been prepared, by our American experience, to believe that civilization festers between opposite poles of plunder and pain. And still, the university waits, unavoidable, at the end of compulsory education, to assure the undisturbed perpetuity of this civilization.

We have learned to suspect and to beware the culture belied by phrases such as "the two-car family," or "job security," or "the Department of Defense," or "law and order." We do not deride the fears of prospering white America. A nation of violence and private property has every reason to dread the violated and the deprived. Its history drives the violated into violence and, one of these days, violence will literally signal the end of violence as a means. We are among those who have been violated into violence. Black American experience staggers away from the resurrecting lord of love. In his place, we must examine the life, through death, of Bigger Thomas. We know he was not paranoid. Crazy, yes. Paranoid, no. We know how his sanity died, and who were his well-educated executioners. And the Black student of his life brims hatred for the hateful choice allowed to Bigger Thomas, hatred for an efficiency that cancels, equally, the humanity of the oppressed and the oppressor. Even so, we confront a continuing tyranny that means Bigger Thomas may yet symbolize the method of our liberation into human community.

How will the American university teach otherwise? One favorite university precept is that of reasonable discourse. We ask, when Bigger Thomas stood there, Black-male-in-white-girl's-bedroom, what did reasonable discourse offer, to him? Who would have listened to his explanation of himself next to the drunken white woman, on her bed?

In America, the traditional routes to Black identity have hardly been normal. Suicide (disappearance by imitation, or willed extinction), violence (hysterical religiosity, crime, armed revolt), and exemplary moral courage; none of these is normal.

And, if we consider humankind, if we consider the origins of human society, we realize that, in America, the traditional routes to white identity have not been normal, either. Identity of person has been pursued through the acquisition of material clues admittedly irrelevant to the achievement of happiness. Identity has been secured among watery objects ceaselessly changing value. Worse, the marketplace has vanquished the workable concept of homeground or, as children say in their games, home-safe.

But Black America has striven toward human community even within the original situation that opposed its development, the situation of slavery. Often enough, at the expense of conceivably better working circumstances, those enslaved pleaded not to be sold away from the extended family they had so desperately scrapped together, inside the slave quarters of a particular plantation. The intensity of Black desiring may be measured when one remembers that legal marriage was forbidden, during slavery. Yet the records boggle full of accounts demonstrating human fealty—as when the freedman saved his earnings over seven or eight years in order to purchase the freedom of his "wife."

Prospering white America perverted, and perverts, the fundamental solace and nurture of community even to the point of derogating the extended family discoverable among America's white and Black impoverished. As any college graduate can tell you, the extended family is "compensation for failure." According to these norms, success happens when the man and his immediate family may competently provide for greater and greater privacy. I.e., greater and greater isolation from others, independence from others, capability to delimit and egotistically control the compass of social experience. Faced by the humanly universal dilemma of individual limit, prospering white America has turned away from the normal plunging into expanded family and commitment. Instead, the pursuit of exclusive power—the power to exclude and to manipulate, plus the pursuit of insulating layers of material shell, have pre-empted the pursuit of community and ridiculed happiness as an invalid, asinine goal.

Blocked by white America, in its questing for community, as the appropriate arena for the appearance and shaping of person, Black America has likewise been blocked in its wayward efforts to emulate the inhumanity of white compensation. Thus, the traditional routes of suicide, violence, and exemplary moral courage have emerged. They have emerged despite the spectacular absence of literature and history to document and support Black life. Or perhaps, precisely because the usual tools a people employ in the determining of identity were strictly prohibited, these alternative, bizarre, and heroic methods devolved.

But community does not form by marriage between martyr and a movie star. The hero is one, and we remain the many. We have begun like objects belonging to the blind. We have spent our generations in a scream that wasted in the golden ear. Giant, demon, clown, angel, bastard, bitch, and, nevertheless, a family longing, we have made it to the gates: Our hearts hungry on the rocks around the countryside, our hopes the same: our hopes: unsatisfied. Now we have the choice, and we must make that choice our own. We are at the gates.

Who are we?

There has been no choosing until now. Until the university, there is no choice. Education is compulsory. Education has paralleled the history of our Black lives; it has been characterized by the punishment of nonconformity, abridgment, withered enthusiasm, distortion, and self-denying censorship. Education has paralleled the life of prospering white America; it has been characterized by reverence for efficiency, cultivation of competence unattended by concern for aim, big white lies, and the mainly successful blackout of Black life.

Black students arrive at the university from somewhere. Where is that, exactly? Where is Black America, all of it, from the beginning? Why do we ask? How does it happen that we do not know?

What is the university, until we arrive? Is it where the teachers of children receive their training? It is where the powerful become more powerful. It is where the norms of this abnormal power, this America, receive the ultimate worship of propagation. It is where the people become usable parts of the whole machine: Machine is not community.

Is the university where the person learns how to become a valuable member of society? Even so, it is not, the university is not where the person learns how he is always a valuable member of an always valuable society of people. It probably takes a college graduate to explain the "higher learning" that does not teach the unearned sanctity and value of each person.

Yet it waits there, at the end of coercion, the citadel of technique and terminology. At the gates, a temporary freedom plays between the student and the school. Choice confronts both sides. It seems. But like the others who have been violated, whose joy has been bled and viciously assaulted, the Black student can choose to refuse the university only at incredible cost. He needs power if he will spring free from dependency upon those who exploit, isolate, and finally destroy. If he will liberate "homebase," he must, for a time, separate himself from the identity of the powerless. No. He must learn to assume the identity of the powerless, in a powerful way. No. He must understand homebase. But where is that? Who is he, this student the university chooses to accept? Does the university have any idea? Fortified by the freaks, the heroes, the saints, the rebels in exile, Black students reject the necessity of miracle, where identity is concerned. Every saint and every rebel of Black America reinforces the determination of the majority to achieve a normal, ordinary access to person. The majority knows it is, by definition, incapable of the miraculous. And yet it admires the consequences of Black miracle in white America: All of us hunt identity.

And so, the Black student enters the gates. Choice of entry is delusional. He must go inside, or perish through dependency. But he rejects the university as it panders to his potential for neither/nor anonymity, or for dysfunctional amnesia. He enters the university and, snatching at the shred reality of freedom-at-last, or first choice, he chooses his family. *The black student clutches at family precisely at that moment when he enters the ultimate glorification of a society that has rejected him. Why is anyone amazed?* Before this moment family has been merely given or else taken away. Finally freed from the obedience, the slavery of childhood, Black students choose a family for the first time:

"When I was a child, I spoke like a child, I thought like a child, I reasoned like a child; when I became a man, I gave up childish ways. For now we see in a mirror dimly, but then face to face. Now I know in part; then I shall understand fully, even as I have been fully understood." From our knees, we have fought tall enough to look into the question of the mirror. More than any other people, we cannot afford to forget the mirror is a questioning. And *face to face*, we eat together in the dining rooms, we dorm together, sleep together, talk together, love ourselves, together, face to face; the family mirror clears inside that chosen clarity. We, Black America, on the prospering white American university campus, we come together as students, Black students. How shall we humanly compose the knowledge that troubles the mind into ideas of life? How can we be who we are?

Black studies. The engineer, the chemist, the teacher, the lawyer, the architect, if he is Black, he cannot honorably engage career except as Black engineer, Black architect. *Of course, he must master the competence, the perspectives of physics, chemistry, economics, and so forth.* But he cannot honorably, or realistically, forsake the origins of his possible person. Or she cannot. Nor can he escape the tyranny of ignorance except as he displaces ignorance with study: study of the impersonal, the amorality of the sciences *anchored by Black Studies*. The urgency of his heart, his breath, demands the knowing of the truth about himself: the truth of Black experience. And so, Black students, looking for the truth, demand teachers least likely to lie, least likely to perpetuate the traditions of lying: lies that deface the father from the memory of the child. We request Black teachers of Black studies. It is not that we believe only Black people can understand the Black experience. It is, rather, that we acknowledge the difference between reality and criticism as the difference between the Host and the Parasite.

As Frantz Fanon has written, the colonized man does not say he knows the truth, he *is* the truth. Likewise, we do not say we know the truth: We are the Truth: We are the living Black experience, and therefore, we are the primary sources of information. For us, there is nothing optional about "Black Experience" and/or "Black Studies": we must know ourselves. But theories and assertions do not satisfy, anymore. Studies are called for. And, regardless how or where these studies lead, the current facts support every effort to create study alliances among nonwhite, or nonprospering white Americans who, all of us, endure as victims of materialism versus our lives.

We look for community. We have already suffered the alternatives to community, to human commitment. We have borne the whiplash of "white studies" unmitigated by the stranger ingredient of humane dedication. Therefore, we cannot, in sanity, pass by the potentiality of Black studies: studies of the person consecrated to the preservation of that person.

On the contrary, "white studies" should do likewise: At this date when humankind enjoys wild facility to annihilate, no human study can sanely ignore the emergency requirements for efficient, yes, competent affirmation of the values of life, and that most precious burden of identity that depends, beggarly, on love.

The university may choose among 1,000 differences of response to Black demands, but if the decision bespeaks the traditional process of majority overrule, white choice will sputter to no effect. Like the rest of America that is no longer willing to endure hostile control, Black America will not accept any choice affecting their lives unless they control even the terms under consideration. And if it is true that Black rejection of majority overrule will lead to a white-predicted "bloodbath," it is also true that he who makes such a prophecy will bear responsibility for its fulfillment.

Poverty is a bloodbath. Exploitation of human life, for material gain, is unforgivable-letting-blood-flow for the sake of other currencies. Perforce, the natural element of Black children has been the American bloodbath. We know American violence, power, and success. Is the university prepared to teach us something new?

Black studies. White studies: Revised. What is the curriculum, what are the standards that only human life threatens to defile and "lower"? Is the curriculum kin to that monstrous metaphor of justice, seated, under blindfold, in an attitude and substance of absolute stone? Life appealing to live, and to be, and to know a community that will protect the living simply because we are alive: This is the menace to university curriculum and standards. This is the possibility of survival we must all embrace: the possibility of life, as has been said, by whatever means necessary.

In New York City, the metaphor of Harlem contains the symbol, and the fact, of City College. On that campus, the most recent miracle of Black America has become a manifest reality. There, Black and Puerto Rican students have joined to issue what they describe as the Fourth Demand. This demand exceeds the scope of lately typical negotiation between school and student. It speaks to community. It reads: "The racial composition of the entering class [is] to reflect the Black and Puerto Rican population of the New York City Schools."

Obviously, the fourth demand reaches outside the University province and into high school habits of student tragedy. In the predominantly Black and Puerto Rican high school nearest City College, the academic diploma rate steadies at 1.2 percent. Since Black and Puerto Rican students constitute the majority of public students, and since the majority of them does not receive an academic diploma, how can the City College reflect their majority status? Either the high schools or the College will have to change almost beyond current planning imagination. To meet the fourth demand, New York City lower schools will have to decide that a 65 percent dropout rate for students, of any color, is intolerable, and that a 1.2 percent academic diploma rate, at any high school, cannot continue.

In fact, how will the City College continue unless it may admit the children of the city? Will the City College of New York resort to importation of students from Iowa and Maine? The children of the city are Black and Puerto Rican; they are the children of suffering and impotence; they are the children coerced into lower grade education that alienates upward of 65 percent of them so that the majority of this majority disappears into varieties of ruin. If the university will not teach, will not instruct the lower schools, by its example, how will they learn? If the university is not the ultimate teaching institution, the ultimate, the most powerful institution to decree the hope of education, per se, what is it? And yet, the City College cries "curriculum" and worries about "standards" even while the future of its conceivable justification, the students of the city schools, disappears except for a self-destructive trace.

Black and Puerto Rican students at the City College, nevertheless, insist upon the fourth demand; they insist upon community. Serving the positive implications of Black Studies (Life Studies), students everywhere must insist on new college admission policies that will guide and accelerate necessary, radical change, at all levels of education. Universities must admit the inequities of the civilization they boast. These inequities mean that the children of Other America have been vanquished by the consequences of compulsory, hostile instruction and inescapable, destructive experience. It is appropriate that the university should literally adopt these living consequences as its own humane privilege, for service. Such embrace waits upon the demonstration of majority conscience. Black America waits upon the demonstration of a conscience that will seek justice with utmost, even ruthless, efficiency.

Yet we do not only wait. Black America moves, headstrong, down toward Damascus. Everybody on the ladder, hanging on identity opposed to the hatred of life. And if we do not name the gods according to the worship of our lives, then what will we worship, in deed?

TWO

7 White English/Black English: The Politics of Translation (1972)

By 1970, in addition to *The Voice of the Children*, I had completed *Who Look at Me, Soulscript, Some Changes*, and *His Own Where*. I had also completed the research and then written the scenario for a half-hour documentary on American slavery that I called *The Crimes of Dollar Blood*. The script was revised, without my permission, and later released by the producers, Milton Meltzer and Doubleday & Company, under the title *Slavery and the Man*.

These works emerged while I was managing full-time responsibilities as Christopher's mother—the proverbial female head of household—and regularly teaching at City College, then Connecticut College, and then Sarah Lawrence College. I was, in fact, by 1970, ready for a serious change of situation.

Toward the end of 1969, Bucky Fuller had urged me to accept the Prix de Rome in Environmental Design, for which he was planning to nominate me. I could not imagine what I would do, or why, or how, outside this country, but his urgings to the effect that a year away, based at the American Academy in Rome, would yield a usefully revised perspective on everything dear to me here finally prevailed.

My novel, *His Own Where*, was the immediate reason for my receiving the Prix de Rome. I wrote it as a means of familiarizing kids with activist principles of urban redesign or, in other words, activist habits of response to environment. I thought to present these ideas within the guise of a Black love story, written entirely in Black English—in these ways I might hope to interest teenagers in reading it.

My projects for the year in Rome were these: To transmute this novel into a scenario for a commercial feature film, and to study alternative urban designs for the promotion of flexible, and pacific, communal street life.

From Rome, I traveled to the Greek island of Mykonos, in January, by myself. It was while I stayed on that cold white island (an island virtually devoid of vegetation) that the idea of land reform in Mississippi came to me.

Mykonos is nothing but a rock. Rowboats carry oranges and meat, and other perishables, into the tiny harbor whenever the sea allows. But if the water becomes too rough, the boats cannot make it to the island and the peoples of Mykonos have to endure a diet consisting mainly of bread, olive oil butter, honey, and coffee, or hot chocolate.

As I walked across and around Mykonos, easily crisscrossing my own steps, I marveled at the clear obduracy of these islanders: Why would anybody settle there, in a place of such inhospitality, a place of no arable land? The vista of sky and sea in Mykonos is stunning, but feeds no one. If the sea permits, the men haul their handwoven, many-times-mended nets out on the waters, and fish. But fish and bread do not constitute a happy routine of nourishment, even supposing you can find either one of these to eat.

A year earlier, in 1969, I had crisscrossed Mississippi, much as I was doing on Mykonos, to write a piece for the *New York Times Magazine* called "Black Home in Mississippi," meeting with leaders and families, everywhere, and driving alone through the long hot roads of the delta. The people of Mississippi, the Black people of Mississippi, especially Dr. Aaron Henry and Mrs. Fannie Lou Hamer, had given me so much, I had wanted to give them something in return, something that might transform the facts of material despair into realistic prospects for an ample, self-sufficient life.

After the publication of the article in the *Times*, Bob Gottlieb at Knopf commissioned me to write a book on Black Mississippi: The idea was to expand upon those interviews and anecdotes, bearing the good news of militant Black determination to remain in Mississippi on newly won terms of freedom and public safety. But that good news was only one facet of the Mississippi situation. Another, equally important dimension of Mississippi life was the fact that the largest number of hunger counties in America were concentrated right there, in Mississippi, one of the most fertile land areas in the United States.

As I stood on the rock of Mykonos, the horrible absurdity of hunger in Mississippi hit me hard: Here, in Mykonos, the people were surviving with dignity where there were no natural support systems for such survival. There, in Mississippi, Black people were perishing from forced dependency and kwashiorkor while bigtime landowners let arable land lie idle, so they could collect government subsidies! Black poverty and hunger in Mississippi were the obscene, absurd consequence of political arrangements whereby private property rights preempted the rights of human beings to life itself.

I cut short my year in Rome and returned to New York City hellbent upon the compilation of a manual for land reform in Mississippi. I finished this in the late spring of 1971 and called the manuscript "More than Enough." The publisher refused to accept it. "Who are you," he asked me, "to write on land reform?"

The hateful shock of this reception threw me into an abyss of rage and depression not much alleviated by the development, that August, of interest from another publisher in underwriting a "fictional" version of the manual. This was to become my second novel, *Okay Now*, which is still unpublished.

But *His Own Where*, meanwhile, was gaining praise and notoriety, both. Black parents in Baltimore joined together to ban the book—a finalist for the N.B.A.—from the public school libraries. Its use of Black English, they reasoned, would encourage their children to shirk the diligent mastery of standard English that college entrance exams and the job market both require. Elsewhere, related objections to the book arose, and this mild furor overtook my own activities. I began meeting with parents and teachers in various circumstances but soon, wearing out on the road and the microphone, I decided to write

61

down my thinking on Black English and let these statements, in general, answer for me.

I published articles on Black English in places as diverse as *Blackstage* and *Leaflet*, the journal for the National Conference of the Teachers of English.

The following essays represent an amalgam of two articles, one of them published in *Publishers Weekly* and the other in *Black World*. (Cf. "Towards a Politics of Language" and "The Politics of Language.")

In 1979, the Michigan courts ruled that Black English is, indeed, an identifiably different language system from that of Standard English and that public schools presuming to teach Black children must present these children with teachers and language studies positively oriented to the distinctive language skills these children bring into the classroom. At last!

WHITE ENGLISH

By now, most Blackfolks—even the most stubbornly duped and desperately light-headed nigger behind his walnut, "anti-poverty" desk—has heard The Man talking that talk, and the necessary translation into Black—*on white terms*—has taken place. Yeah. The Man has made his standard English speech, his second inaugural address, his budget statements, and ain' no body left who don't understand the meaning of them words falling out that mouth: In the *New York Times*, February 25, 1973, Dick Nixon has described the genocide perpetrated by America in Vietnam as *"one of the most unselfish missions ever undertaken by one nation in the defense of another."*

Now, you just go ahead and let any little Black child lead you to the truth behind that particular, monstrous lie: let him tell you about the twelve days of Christmas "carpet bombing," My Lai, day-by-day incineration of human lives, the mining of rivers, the bombing of hospitals, and "defoliation" of the land, over there. They all—all of them whitefolks ruling the country— they all talk that talk, that "standard (white) English." It is the language of the powerful. Language is political. That's why you and me, my Brother and my Sister, that's why we sposed to choke our natural self into the weird, lying, barbarous, unreal, white speech and writing habits that the schools lay down like holy law. Because, in other words, the powerful don't play; they mean to keep that power, and those who are the powerless (you and me) better shape up—mimic/ape/suck—in the very image of the powerful, or the powerful will destroy you—you and our children.

Dick Nixon has declared that, since the U.S. of A. has completed its "unselfish mission" in Vietnam, America can turn "more fully to the works of compassion, concern and social progress at home." Sounds pretty good, right? Translation: He means the death of all human welfare programs to end hunger, hazardous housing, inequity in court, injustice, and the suffering of poor health. Check it out; I'm not lying to you. Standard English use of the word "compassion" actually means the end of milk programs for needy school kids, an 18-month halt to every form of federal assistance for low-income new housing/ rehabilitation, the terminating of Community Action Programs across the nation, and the subtraction of federal aid from elementary and junior high and high school systems especially intended to enable impoverished youngsters. And, since that's what "compassion" means in White English, I most definitely do not see why any child should learn *that* English/prize it/ participate in this debasement of this human means to human community: this debasement of language, per se.

See, the issue of white English is inseparable from the issues of mental health and bodily survival. If we succumb to phrases such as "winding down the war," or if we accept "pacification" to mean the murdering of unarmed villagers, and "self-reliance" to mean bail money for Lockheed Corporation and bail money for the mis-managers of the Pennsylvania Railroad, on the one hand, but also, if we allow "self-reliance" to mean starvation and sickness and misery for poor families, for the aged, and for the permanently disabled/permanently discriminated against —then our mental health is seriously in peril: we have entered the world of doublespeak-bullshit, and our lives may soon be lost behind that entry. In any event, The Man has brought the war home, where it's always really been at: sometimes explosive, sometimes smoldering, but currently, as stark, inhuman, and deliberate as the "perfect grammar" of Nixon's war cries raised, calm as a killer, against the weak, the wanting, and the ones who cannot fight back: How will we survive this new—this, to use a standard English term, "escalated"—phase of white war against Black life?

Well, first let me run down some of the ways we will *not* survive:

1. We will not survive by joining the game according to the rules set up by our enemies; we will not survive by imitating the doublespeak/bullshit/nonthink standard English of the powers that be: Therefore, if the F.B.I. asks you do you know so-and-so, a member of the Black Panther Party, for example, you will *not* respond in this Watergate "wise": "I do seem to recall having had some association with the person in question during, or should I say, sometime during, the past." You will say, instead, for example: "What's it to you? What do I look like to you? What right do you have to ask me that question?"

2. We will *not* try to pretend that we are the Pennsylvania Railroad or some enormous, profiteering corporation such as Grumman Aerospace, and consider the government pennies to "small businesses" initiated by "minority businessmen" to be anything other than what they are: pennies copping out on the mass situation of increasing disparity between the white Have-group and the Black Have-nots.

3. We will not help ourselves into extinction by deluding our Black selves into the belief that we should/can become white, that we can/should sound white, think white because then we will be *like* the powerful and therefore we will *be* powerful: that is just a terrible, sad joke: you cannot obliterate yourself and do anything else, whatever, let alone be powerful: that is a logical impossibility; we must cease this self-loathing delusion and recognize that power and happiness and every good thing that we want and need and deserve must come to us as we truly are: must come to us, a Black people, on our terms, re-

64

specting our definitions of our goals, our choice of names, our styles of speech, dress, poetry, and jive. Otherwise, clearly, the "victory" is pyrrhic. You have won a job, you think, because you have "successfully" hidden away your history—your mother and your father and the man or woman that you love and *how* you love them, *how* you dance that love, and sing it. That is victory by obliteration of the self. That is not survival.

4. We will not survive unless we realize that we remain jeopardized, as a people, by a fully conscious political system to annihilate whoever/whatever does not emulate its mainstream vocabulary, values, deceit, arrogance, and killer mentality. This is a time when those of us who believe in people, first, must become political, in every way possible: we must devise and pursue every means for survival as the people we are, as the people we want to become. Therefore, when a magazine like *Newsweek* has the insolence to ask, on its cover: WHATEVER HAPPENED TO BLACK AMERICA?, we must be together, ready, and strong to answer, on our own terms, on our own *political* terms: none of your goddamned business; you know, anyway; you did it; you stripped the programs; you ridiculed/ humiliated the poor; you laughed when we wept: don't ask: we gone make you *answer* for this shit.

White power uses white English as a calculated, political display of power to control and eliminate the powerless. In America, that power belongs to white power. School, compulsory public school education, is the process whereby Black children first encounter the punishing force of this white power. "First grade" equals first contact with the politics of white language, and its incalculably destructive consequences for Black lives. This is what I mean, exactly: both Black and white youngsters are compelled to attend school. Once inside this system, the white child is rewarded for mastery of his standard, white English: the language he learned at his mother's white and standard knee. But the Black child is punished for mastery of his non-standard, Black English; for the ruling elite of America have decided that *non*-standard is *sub*-standard, and even dangerous, and must be eradicated. Moreover, the white child re-

65

ceives formal instruction in his standard English, and endless opportunities for the exercise and creative display of his language. But where is the elementary school course in Afro-American language, and where are the opportunities for the *accredited* exercise, and creative exploration, of Black language? The two languages are not interchangeable. They cannot, nor do they attempt to communicate equal or identical thoughts, or feelings. And, since the experience to be conveyed is quite different, Black from white, these lingual dissimilarities should not surprise or worry anyone. However, they are both communication systems with regularities, exceptions, and values governing their word designs. Both are equally liable to poor, good, better, and creative use. In short, they are both accessible to critical criteria such as clarity, force, message, tone, and imagination. Besides this, standard English is comprehensible to Black children, even as Black language is comprehensible to white teachers—supposing that the teachers are willing to make half the effort they demand of Black students.

Then what is the difficulty? The problem is that we are saying *language*, but really dealing with power. The word "standard" is just not the same as the word "technical" or "rural" or "straight." *Standard* means the rule, the norm. Anyone deviating from the standard is therefore "wrong." As a result, literally millions of Black children are "wrong" from the moment they begin to absorb and imitate the language of their Black lives. Is that an acceptable idea?

As things stand, childhood fluency in Afro-American language leads to reading problems that worsen, course failure in diverse subjects dependent on reading skills, and a thoroughly wounded self-esteem. Afterward, an abject school career is eclipsed by an abject life career. "Failing" white English leads straight to a "failure" of adult life. This, I submit, is a fundamental, nationwide experience of Black life up against white English used to destroy us: literally accept the terms of the oppressor, or perish: that is the irreducible, horrifying truth of the politics of language.

Well, number one, we grownups: we, the Black mothers and Black fathers, and Black teachers, and Black writers, and grown

Blackfolk, in general: we do not have to let this damnable situation continue; we must make it stop. We cannot accept the terms, the language of our enemy and expect to win anything; we cannot accept the coercion of our children into failure and expect to survive, as a people. The legitimacy of our language must be fully acknowledged by all of us. That will mean insisting that white/standard English be presented simply as the Second Language. That will mean presenting the second language, obviously, with perpetual reference to the first language, and the culture the first language bespeaks.

Sincere recognition of Black language as legitimate will mean formal instruction and encouragement in its use, within the regular curriculum. It will mean the respectful approaching of Black children, *in the language of Black children.* Yes: it's true that we need to acquire competence in the language of the currently powerful: Black children in America must acquire competence in white English, for the sake of self-preservation: BUT YOU WILL NEVER TEACH A CHILD A NEW LANGUAGE BY SCORNING AND RIDICULING AND FORCIBLY ERASING HIS FIRST LANGUAGE.

We can and we ought to join together to protect our Black children, our Black language, our terms of our reality, and our defining of the future we dream and desire. The public school is one, ready-made battleground. But the war is all around us and the outcome depends on how we understand or fail to perceive the serious, political intention to homogenize us, Blackfolks, out of existence. In our daily, business phone calls, in our "formal" correspondence with whites, in what we publish let us dedicate ourselves to the revelation of our true selves, on our given terms, and demand respect for us, as we are. Let us study and use our Black language, more and more: it is not A Mistake, or A Verbal Deficiency. It is a communication system subsuming dialect/regional variations that leave intact, nevertheless, a language that is invariable in profound respects. For example:

A. Black language practices minimal inflection of verb forms. (E.g.: *I go, we go, he go,* and *I be, you be,* etc.) This is *non-*

standard and, also, an obviously more logical use of verbs. It is also evidence of a value system that considers the person—the actor—more important than the action.

B. Consistency of syntax:

You going to the store.   (Depending on tone, can be a question.)

You going to the store.   (Depending: can be a command.)

You going to the store.   (Depending: can be a simple, declarative statement.)

C. Infrequent, irregular use of the possessive case.

D. Clear, logical use of multiple negatives within a single sentence, to express an unmistakably negative idea. E.g., You ain gone bother me no way no more, you hear?

E. Other logical consistencies, such as: *ours, his, theirs,* and, therefore, *mines.*

Our Black language is a political fact suffering from political persecution and political malice. Let us understand this and meet the man, politically; let us meet the man *talking the way we talk;* let us not fail to seize this means to our survival, despite white English and its power. Let us condemn white English for what it is: a threat to mental health, integrity of person, and persistence as a people of our own choosing.

And, as for our children: let us make sure that the whole world will welcome and applaud and promote the words they bring into our reality; in the struggle to reach each other, there can be no right or wrong words for our longing and our needs; there can only be the names that we trust and we try.

BLACK ENGLISH

As a poet and writer, I deeply love and I deeply hate words. I love the infinite evidence and change and requirements and possibilities of language; every human use of words that is joyful, or honest, or new because experience is new, or old because each personal history testifies to inherited pleasures and/or inherited, collective memories of peril, pain, and even genocide.

As a human being, I delight in this miraculous, universal means of communion: I rejoice in this communing means that leading linguists, such as Noam Chomsky, have now shown to be innate, rather than learned; thanks to the revolutionary work of such linguists, we now understand that word patterns connecting person to reality, and reflecting and/or responding to reality, are no more learned than the brain is learned or the intestine is learned: language is a communal means intrinsic to human life. And I celebrate this fact of language that man and womankind have been privileged to explore and extend always as a means of discovery and/or revelation and of coming together and/or reaching closer to social conditions that will justify and summon forth the lyrical, hallelujah telegrams of love and peace and victory for merciful, just, and life-supporting human conduct.

But, as a Black poet and writer, I hate words that cancel my name and my history and the freedom of my future: I hate the words that condemn and refuse the language of my people in America; I am talking about a language deriving from the Niger-Congo congeries of language. I am talking about a language that joins with the Russian, Hungarian, and Arabic languages, among others, in its elimination of what technicians call a "present copula"—a verb interjected between subject and predicate. Or, to break that down a bit: I am talking about a language where I will tell you simply that, "*They mine.*" (And, incidentally, if I tell you "*they mine,*" you don't have no kind of trouble understanding exactly what I mean, do you?)

As a Black poet and writer, I am proud of our Black, verbally bonding system born of our struggle to avoid annihilation—as Afro-American self, Afro-American marriage, community, and Afro-American culture. I am proud of this language that our continuing battle just *to be* has brought into currency. And so I hate the arrogant, prevailing rejection of this, our Afro-American language. And so I work, as a poet and writer, against the eradication of this system, this language, this carrier of Black-survivor consciousness.

But we are talking about power, and poetry and books—history books, novels, what have you—none of these can win against the schools, the teachers, the media, the fearful parents, and the ruling elite of this country, unless we understand the politics of language. In America, the politics of language, the willful debasement of this human means to human communion has jeopardized the willingness of young people to believe anything they hear or read—even if it's just the time of day.

And what is anybody going to do about it? I suggest that, for one, we join forces to cherish and protect our various, multifoliate lives against pacification, homogenization, the silence of terror, and surrender to standards that despise and disregard the sanctity of each and every human life. We can begin by looking at language. Because it brings us together, as folks, because it makes known the unknown strangers we otherwise remain to each other, language is a process of translation; and a political process, taking place on the basis of who has the power to use, abuse, accept or reject the words—the lingual messages we must attempt to transmit—to each other and/or against each other.

In short, the subject of "Black English" cannot be intelligently separate from the subject of a language as translation and translation as a political process distinguishing between the powerless and the powerful, in no uncertain terms. Here are a few facts to illustrate my meaning:

1. Apparently, "Black English" needs defense even though it is demonstrably a language; a perfectly adequate, verbal means of communication that can be understood by anyone but the most outrightly, retarded, standard racist.

2. On the other hand, where is the defense, who among the standard, grammatical, white English mainstreamers feels the need, even, to defend his imposition of his language on me and my children?

3. Thou know'st the mask of night is on my face,
   Else would a maiden blush bepaint my cheek
   For that which thou hast heard me speak tonight.

Fain would I dwell on form, fain, fain deny
what I have spoke: but farewell compliment:
Dost thou love me? I know thou wilt say "Ay"
And I will take thy word: yet, if thou swear'st,
Thou mayst prove false: at lovers' perjuries,
They say, Jove laughs.

Romeo and Juliet (Act 2, Scene 2)

Now that ain hardly standard English. But just about every kid forced into school has to grapple with that particular rap. Why? Because the powers that control the language that controls the process of translation have decided that *Romeo and Juliet* is *necessary*, nay, *indispensable*, to passage through compulsory, public school education.

4. "You be different from the dead. All them tombstones tearing up the ground, look like a little city, like a small Manhattan, not exactly. Here is not the same. Here, you be bigger than the buildings, bigger than the little city. You be really different from the rest, the resting other ones.

"Moved in his arms, she make him feel like smiling. Him, his head an Afro-bush spread free beside the stones, headstones thinning in the heavy air. Him, a ready father, public lover, privately at last alone with her, with Angela, a half an hour walk from the hallway where they start out to hold themselves together in the noisy darkness, kissing, kissed him, kissed her, kissing.

"Cemetery let them lie there belly close, their shoulders now undressed down to the color of the heat they feel, in lying close, their legs a strong disturbing of the dust. His own where, own place for loving made for making love, the cemetery where nobody guard the dead."
His Own Where

Now that ain no kind of standard English, neither. Both excerpts come from love stories about white and Black teenagers, respectively. But the Elizabethan, nonstandard English of *Romeo and Juliet* has been adjudged, by the powerful, as something students should tackle and absorb. By contrast, the Black, nonstandard language of my novel, *His Own Where*, has been adjudged, by the powerful, as substandard and even injurious to young readers.

I am one among a growing number of Black poets and writers dedicated to the preservation of Black language within our lives, and dedicated to the health of our children as they prepare themselves for life within this standard, white America which has despised even our speech and our prayers and our love. As long as we shall survive, Black, in white America, we, and our children, require and deserve the power of Black language, Black history, Black literature, as well as the power of standard English, standard history, and standard literature. To the extent that Black survival fails on these terms, it will be a political failure: it will be the result of our not recognizing and not revolting against the political use of language, to extinguish the people we want to be and the people we have been. Politics is power. Language is political. And language, its reward, currency, punishment, and/or eradication—is political in its meaning and in its consequence.

A few days ago, a white woman telephoned to ask me to appear on her television program: she felt free to tell me that if I sounded "Black" then she would not "hire" me. This is what I am trying to say to you: language is power. And that woman is simply one of the ruling powerful people in white America who feel free to reject and strangle whoever will not mimic them—in language, values, goals. In fact, I answered her in this way: You are a typical racist. And that is the political truth of the matter, as I see it, as I hope you will begin to see it: for no one has the right to control and sentence to poverty anyone —because he or she is different and proud and honest in his or her difference and his or her pride.

Let me end by focusing on Black language, per se: A young friend of mine went through some scarifying times, leaving her homeless. During this period of intense, relentless dread and abuse, she wrote poems, trying to cope. Here are two lines from her poetry: "what have life meanted to me" and, "you are forgotten you use to existed." There is no adequate, standard English translation possible for either expression of her spirit. They are intrinsically Black language cries of extreme pain so telling that even the possibilities of meaning and existence have been formulated in a past tense that is emphatic, severe. I deeply hope that more of us will want to learn and protect Black language. If we lose our fluency in our language, we may irreversibly forsake elements of the spirit that have provided for our survival.

8 American Violence and the Holy Loving Spirit (1972)

"American Violence" is an excerpt from the unpublished manual for land reform, "More than Enough."

It was the 36th Annual Conference of Southern Governors, in Gulfport, Mississippi. They'd all be there. And for days before the Conference began, Mississippi's Governor, John Bell Williams, publicly promised a strong, united stand against school busing and other, defamatory inroads on the character of Deep South Status Quo.

Gulfport is the southern boundary, the end, of mississippi-america. After this town, there are simply waves of open water that commingle, slosh, idle briefly, and then ebb loose, uncertainly, again, away from the edge of America that is sand.

On a Sunday, I drove down to Gulfport during the Governors' Conference. I wanted to see one limit to mississippi-america, an ending of it that would be beautiful, and that would be, by its very nature, liberating/free-form as the ocean is.

And I wanted to see an absolutely southernmost, Mississippi town on its Governors' best, Sunday-dressed-up behavior.

The day was fine: hot, clear, and the road, the highway, was empty, for miles and miles and miles. So was the bordering countryside: empty for miles and miles and miles.

Nearing Gulfport on 49S, you could still see evidence of Hurricane Camille: twisted-around and twisted-down palm and pine trees alternating snapped with fractured tree trunks. There were also large, prominent structures warped and pulled apart, as by a terrible, great fire, except that the remains were not discolored.

49S turns into 25th Street, the main drag of Gulfport. From there you glimpse extremely small, extremely packed-together houses that look more like one-room, emergency huts. This is Black Gulfport. Along the sides of 25th Street, in downtown proper, functional, dusty storefronts intersperse with ramshackle or deserted, commercial space. It is like an old dress for sale.

I am trying to maintain a car's length behind five or six white teenagers on motorcycles, with Alabama license plates. They are playing a game to test my agility at the wheel, and the speed of my foot from brake pedal to the accelerator.

I would pull over, and wait them out, except that everything is closed, and here, in the center of town, there are no Black people in sight.

We, the motorcycles and I, turn left, on 90 East, which proves to be a four-lane, beach drive, divided in half by a strip of grass and palm trees. On one side, there is the sea, after a narrow white beach, and on the other side, there are imposing, sea-view homes and motels that try to lend the place an appearance of prosperity.

There are no Black people on the beach or in the water.

To check how hot it is, I switch off the air conditioner; sweat forms all over me, running from my scalp and through my toes, and down my face, and into my eyes. I am drenched, and look at the water where nobody Black is swimming. It is a light brown, barely blue color, with a sideways current, moving westward under a frugal foam: no waves.

At 30 to 40 mph, the traffic rolls from Gulfport into Biloxi, following the shoreline. Now we pass by several sailboats. I head toward a curved-shed marina where a leisurely looking crowd seems to be. It will probably be a good place to get a cold drink. I pull in among the other, parked cars; it will be a relief to stop driving, drink something cold, and look around. Scan the people: nobody Black; change my mind; turn around, and head back to Gulfport, taking 90 West, this time.

Where is everybody?

The Holiday Inn is not doing a lot of business. While I stop there to make a phone call, one of the dining room waitresses calls over to someplace else, where the Governors are staying, and asks if they could use her help.

It really is Sunday in Mississippi. Except for the engines of the cars, there is complete silence. The heat is hypnotic.

You get into line with your car and just roll along slowly like a sweat bead under the sun. So I am back in line, and rolling like sweat between two other, sun-shining cars.

On the beach, one or two white girls wearing bikinis stroll along languidly with their boyfriends, but there is no sound.

Blue-and-white striped, red-and-white striped, whirling toys spin, vertiginous, and very bright, and high, in the air.

Color is the only solid thing in this heat: the only thing to catch your eye, and keep you awake, naming words to yourself, like *red, green, blue.*

Everything else wriggles blurred in the sweat of the silent day.

We have rolled to a red light.

From the cab of a truck two cars up ahead, a bare-backed white man jumps down.

He comes toward us, running, it seems, to pick up an object that has fallen from his truck. It looks like a piece of pipe, or a muffler. The object lies about fifteen feet ahead of my car, on my left. He's probably running so he won't miss the green light. In this heat, it seems peculiar, almost comical to watch somebody running.

He is naked from the waist up, and wearing gold corduroy trousers with a black belt. He is muscular and fat, and his brown hair looks like a crew cut growing in.

The whole scene progresses like a steamy, well-lit slow motion film.

As the runner nears, the blue Chevrolet just to my left starts up fast, and frightens the man.

The man, the runner, darts to the grass divider, for safety. The blue car swerves up and onto the divider so it can clip and kill him. Boomp.

The car catches the runner; hits him slow; he hurtles way above our heads.

The car seems to wait for him. Just as the man's body touches down on the hood of the car, the car jerks forward, catapulting the body onto the top of the car: Bounce.

He lands on the ground. The car backs over the body. Then the car jerks forward and off the divider and then, but slowly, rolls ahead to the next light.

Around me, women and children scream weak in the hot, watery air.

The man rises from the ground; his back and chest are streaming blood.

He completes his run to the object on the ground. Picks it up. None of us moves. We are watching him.

The blue Chevrolet has rolled on, slowly, out of sight.

The runner rounds the front of his truck like a dogged, champion retriever, and as though his bones are falling apart from his flesh.

Nothing happens.

Then the driver of the yellow car to my left, he slams out of his car and races over to the man and has to wrestle him to a halt. The dying man is in shock.

Now covered with blood himself, the driver carries the runner back toward his own car full of children and women who are no longer screaming.

No one moves.

We have witnessed a murder.

We wait.

My eyes burn. The tears and the sweat mix bitterly, and this, the first murder I have seen, in mississippi-america, it is white on white, on a Sunday.

No one moves. We have all been hurt.

We are all terrified.

9   Whose Burden? (1974)

On my second journey into Mississippi I stayed with Mrs.
Fannie Lou Hamer and her husband, Pap, immediately following the drunken murder of Joetha Collier, the young Black girl
shot down by white beer-drinking teenagers on the afternoon
of her graduation from high school. When her body was
found, Joetha's hand still held her diploma.

Mrs. Hamer was intent upon arousing a response of national
outrage to this killing, and for this reason her house was
under siege. Cars of white men would cruise by, firing at the
windows and the porch. It was during this visit that Mrs.
Fannie Lou told me the story of her life so that I could create
a children's biography to broadcast the courage and love of
her political commitment. She was, in many ways, a mother to
me: protective, earthy, fearless, and blessed by an hilarious
and deadpan sense of humor.

Around this time I also completed a comparative analysis
of Reconstruction and the Civil Rights Era, which I wrote
in the form of a Black English dialog between two Black boys.
This was called "Dry Victories."

Even though I was still stung and disgusted by some excesses
of the Black nationalist movement at the end of the sixties—
disgusted at the Stalinist purge sessions during which Black
folks sat around criticizing each other for being "incorrect" or
"not Black enough," by 1973, I had become a nationalist in
thought and feeling, both.

When I read about the African famine in the Sahel, for

example, it was my stubborn idea that an exclusively Black national action should be organized to save those starving peoples whom we were pleased to describe in our daily rhetoric as "our brothers and our sisters." This would affirm our coming of age in that we would no longer ask for help; we would help ourselves.

To this purpose, I joined with Inez Smith Reid, then Executive Director of the Black Women's Community Development Fund, to erect an overnight crusade that we called Afro-Americans Against the Famine.

According to U.N. reports, ten million Africans would die, by September, if massive rescue infusions of food did not reach the interior of the Sahel.

Inez and I called a national meeting of Black media peoples at the Negro Ensemble Company in early July, 1973. It was well attended. Jesse Jackson flew in from Chicago. Carlos Russell moderated the proceedings and, by voice acclamation, I was appointed National Coordinator of AAAF. Inez was appointed the national spokesperson. Our goals included a saturation publicity effort to familiarize the national Black community with the African crisis, the establishment of an effective African lobby in Washington, and the delivery of rescue foods, in adequate quantities, to the Sahel.

Given the September deadline projected by the United Nations, AAAF was an emergency task force operating without sleep, money, opportunities for second thought, or room for factional conflict. We sought to activate the broadest possible coalition of Black leaders and peoples. Notably, Roberta Flack donated a radio spot publicizing the famine and the various means that were being used to assist its termination.

At the climax of this attempt, we held an August benefit at the Apollo Theatre. Among those who gave of their time and spirit, in the flesh, were Mrs. Fannie Lou Hamer, Andrew Young, John Hendrik Clarke, and Betty Carter. Brothers from Attica volunteered to safeguard the performers, the speakers, and the monies raised that night.

Altogether, that was an exhausting, instructive, and unsuccessful campaign, to my mind. So many people resisted the appeal for action! It was as though Black nationalism meant only a preoccupation with your neighborhood conditions, a preoccupation incapable of making pragmatic connections to the continental African struggle. AAAF raised some consciousness, some monies, but no effective African lobby was formed and an effective African lobby still does not exist.

It was then that my own ideas began to change, once again. It seemed to be true, like it or not, that skin was not enough: That color is not enough to save your life. Certainly it is quite enough to kill you.

To this last point, the DeFunis case (DeFunis alleged that he was not accepted in law school as the result of reverse discrimination which, his attorneys in the case argued, was the practical meaning of affirmative action) soon sent white editors into a competition, nationwide: Who could publish the most telling white perspective on this controversy? Nowhere was there evidence of an effort to publish a Black perspective on this, the "reverse discrimination" predecessor to Bakke.

When the DeFunis case broke, I was living in Washington, D.C., with a young Black woman in her last year at law school. She and the handful of other Black law students at Georgetown University looked in vain for national publication of the opposite view, the view that would reassure the future of affirmative action policies.

My weekly *New Republic* arrived, carrying a piece by the white attorney Nathan Lewin entitled "Which Man's Burden?" Writing in support of the DeFunis position, Lewin conjured up a situation of particular distress to Jewish applicants to law school. Apparently the villains responsible for all of this putative onus were none other than Black law students who, according to the U.S. Commission on Civil Rights in 1977, accounted for all of 4.7 *percent* of the total enrollment in first degree legal studies.

Yet another national publication had seen fit to release the statements of only one side of what was everywhere acknowledged to be a controversy!

When I called the *New Republic* to inquire whether or not they intended to solicit a statement from someone such as

Eleanor Holmes Norton or Lennox Hinds (then head of the National Conference of Black Lawyers) and learned that they did not, I sat down to my typewriter and vented my anger.

Then I got on my bike and rode over to the offices of the *New Republic*, barging in with considerable, building malice. I handed my letter to the only editor I could find, and let him understand that I truly believed that he should and that, therefore, he *would* solicit a pro-affirmative action statement and then print it, the other side of the debate.

To my astonishment, next week's *New Republic* arrived, carrying my letter as though it had been solicited/submitted as an article.

Among other things, if I had known they were going to run this piece, I would have titled it, *What Burden?*

Judging from the frequency with which Black subjects—from political to artistic—receive any attention on your pages, and judging from the frequency with which Black viewpoint on any subject, Black/white/national/international has appeared within your publication, you do not deem Black readership an important part of your support. Nevertheless, judging from the frequency with which you allude to the moral dimensions of various issues and/or the strictly moral considerations of this or that public personality's behavior, you do regard moral responsibility as a valid and preferably operable concept in the conduct of one's affairs: I speak, then, to the moral irresponsibility of your editorial conduct as demonstrated by your choosing to publish Nathan Lewin's piece, "Which Man's Burden?" (May 4, 1974). Given the conceivably devastating, multimillionfold implications of the DeFunis case, and inasmuch as your chosen writer, Lewin himself, elects to reduce the issue substantially to a question of Jewish rights versus Black need, it seems altogether indefensible on your part that you have not published *two* statements simultaneously: one Black, and one Jewish. Instead you have published a decidedly partisan opinion and response on this unmistakably controversial question, and that opinion has been solicited from someone naturally representing the interests of only one of the allegedly aggrieved interest groups: Jewish interests.

Moreover, Lewin writes under the title you have allowed: "Which Man's Burden?"—which title is unspeakably offensive and, as a matter of fact, even shocking. The title clearly predicates that we, Black people, *are* the burden of white men, and that the sole question for consideration is *which* white man's burden. Now if you imagine that such an insolent pair of assumptions coincides with the most entirely sober, contemporary and historic Black testimony regarding the burdens of Black life enjoined to survive inside a contemptuous and exploitative, hostile, white society, then even your imaginations suffer from extreme mistaking of the facts.

Several declarations contained by Lewin's piece deserve full challenge. I will limit myself, however, to a consideration of only two which finally interlink as a partisan postulation promising enormous, unconscionable harm if not refuted.

Lewin purports to present a summary of "affirmative action" policies: their origins and consequences. At one point, he avows that such programs proved onerous to whites: "There was, however, a disquieting sameness to the groups that were being asked to bear the burden."

1. Is Lewin surprised, does he wish to elicit an expression of surprise at the "finding" (actually a Lewin assertion unaccompanied by substantiating, factual data) that those who *have* something will at least resent being asked to share it with those who have been denied the same?

2. What follows from the assertion that the "onus" of Black admission where formerly we have been denied, was inequitably distributed among whites? Are benefits/privileges/powers equitably distributed among whites? Why should alleged burdens be any more equitably distributed among whites than benefits? And, if there is a prevailing white American situation of inequities among whites, then who is responsible for that? Is the powerless, allegedly burdensome Black man responsible? DeFunis directly addresses the possible or impossible life ex-

perience of too many millions of Black lives for less than fair discussion.

Elsewhere your spokesman Lewin asserts: "Again, a critical question is: who should pay to correct society's maladjustment. At this point Jewish groups, representing a community that had suffered discrimination and found a refuge in certain professions and in the universities, complained—*with substantial justification*—[my italics] that an excessive share of the costs of repair comes out of the Jewish community."

1. Black people, including Black students, have found no "refuge" anywhere here in white America.

2. Lewin inadmissibly licenses himself by taking the DeFunis case, an issue of academic admissions policies in the context of "affirmative action" goals, beyond that context into an aggrieved netherland "policed by federal officials" (!) where Blacks rise by stepping on the necks of their Jewish compatriots.

That is a lurid, misleading, inflammatory blow-up of the issue, and a willful mockery of the facts. For example, if we look carefully at the Jewish-Black polarization that took place in the light of the New York City public school system, then we see that that crisis did not represent an instance where Jews shared an "excessive" cost of the White Man's Burden. Rather, the crisis made plain a tragic instance where the human and social situation had changed complexion and ethnicity, while the political/powerful factors ruling that situation had *not* changed accordingly. The result was extreme conflict—not burden—but legitimate conflict of interests.

3. But bringing DeFunis back where it belongs, in the center of this discussion: *I request the factual presenting of the "substantial justification" for Jewish "complaint" regarding Jewish presence in law schools across the country versus black: I request a factual, comparative presentation within a given framework of proportional representation for each group, on a national basis.* Afterward, I trust you will forego further racist slur and lamentation.

10 Notes Toward a Black Balancing of Love and Hatred (1974)

When I received an unexpected invitation to teach at Yale, I was surprised because I knew no one on the English or the Afro-American Studies faculty. But, by 1974, teaching no longer seemed to me an accident, a stunt, or primarily a distraction from my real work as a poet. Teaching had begun to alter even the way I approached things as a writer. The vast innocence of my students, Black and white, signified a vulnerability that I became increasingly determined not to violate with endless bad news.

And it is not possible really to teach both Black and white students but to sustain a loving commitment only to some of them. This fact began to change my conception of the community I wanted my lifework to encompass. I found myself becoming self-consciously concerned to dent the extremely low self-esteem, and the commonplace sense of impotence, that seriously disfigured the formulating worldview of my students, regardless of race.

To be sure, I attempted to identify elements of responsibility in different ways, depending upon whether we were examining questions of white or Black experience in American history. I mean, if there is slavery then there are two factors, two realms of responsibility, at least. And if you teach the descendants of slavery, the descendants of the slaves as well as the descendants of the slaveowners, then you have a double obligation to try and illuminate what happened by considering the implications of what did *not* occur, or what continues *not* to occur.

But teaching at Yale was special, as it turned out. There I encountered every traditional orthodoxy imaginable so that, as a kind of flamboyant affirmation, rain or shine, I made myself wear very high heels. Let the hallowed halls echo to the fact of a woman, a Black woman, passing through!

Somewhat in the same state of mind, the overwhelming reverence for Richard Wright in the Afro-American Studies Department to the exclusion of other important Black writers truly got on my nerves. Besides, the exclusive emphasis upon Black men in Afro-American Studies exactly mirrors the exclusive emphasis upon white men that you meet, relentlessly, in "white studies."

About a year and a half before I went to teach at Yale, my friend Alice Walker spent a weekend at my home. We talked ourselves hoarse, as usual, and one of the things Alice insisted upon was my need to read Hurston's *Their Eyes Were Watching God*, without delay. She put a copy of the novel in my hand, as she boarded the train back to the city. I went home and spent a night, including thunderstorms, mesmerized by this fantastic writer. But, at Yale, Zora Neale Hurston was Zora Neale Who?

So I wrote these "Notes Toward a Black Balancing of Love and Hatred." The piece was published in *Black World*, 1974.

As I reread this essay, tonight, what seems to me as pressing as the need to honor both Hurston and Wright is the need to abhor and defy definitions of Black heritage and Black experience that suggest we are anything less complicated, less unpredictable, than the whole world.

We should take care so that we will lose none of the jewels of our soul. We must begin, now, to reject the white, either/or system of dividing the world into unnecessary conflict. For example, it is tragic and ridiculous to choose between Malcolm X and Dr. King: each of them hurled himself against a quite different aspect of our predicament, and both of them, literally, gave their lives to our ongoing struggle.

We need everybody and all that we are. We need to know and make known the complete, constantly unfolding, complicated heritage that is our Black experience. We should absolutely resist the superstar, one-at-a-time mentality that threatens the varied and resilient, flexible wealth of our Black future, even as it shrinks and obliterates incalculable segments of our history.

In Black literature, we have lost many jewels to the glare of white, mass-media manipulation. According to whitepower, Ralph Ellison was the only Black novelist writing, in this country, while whitepower "allowed" his star to shine. Then, the media "gave" us James Baldwin—evidently all by himself. And then there was *only* Eldridge Cleaver. (Remember him?)

But towering before and above these media-isolated giants, there was always Richard Wright. He has been presented as a solitary figure on the literary landscape of his period. But, right along with him, and six years his senior, there was Zora Neale Hurston. And the fact is that we almost lost Zora to the choose-between games played with Black Art; until recently, no one had ever heard of her; certainly, no one read her books. And yet, anyone who has dipped into her work, even once, will tell you: the long-term obscurity of her joy and wisdom is an appalling matter of record. So we would do well to carefully reconsider these two, Hurston and Wright. Perhaps that will let us understand the cleavage in their public reception, and prevent such inequity and virtual erasure from taking place, again.

Each of them achieved unprecedented, powerful, and extremely important depths of Black vision and commitment, in their lifework; according to the usual criteria, they were both Great Writers. Yet, while Richard Wright spawned many, many followers, and enjoyed the rewards of well-earned fame, Zora Neale Hurston suffered through devastating critical and popular neglect, inspired no imitators, and finally died, penniless, and was buried in an unmarked grave. Why did this happen?

I believe we were misled into the notion that *only one kind* of writing—protest writing—and that *only one kind* of protest writing—deserves our support and study.

A few years back, Hoyt Fuller posed the primary functions of Protest and Affirmation as basic to an appreciation of Black Art. Wright's *Native Son* is widely recognized as the prototypical, Black, protest novel. By comparison, Hurston's novel, *Their Eyes Were Watching God*, seems to suit, perfectly, the obvious connotations of Black affirmation.

But I would add that the functions of protest and affirmation are not, ultimately, distinct: that, for instance, affirmation of Black values and lifestyle within the American context is, indeed, an act of protest. Therefore, Hurston's affirmative work is profoundly defiant, just as Wright's protest unmistakably asserts our need for an alternative, benign environment. We have been misled to discount the one in order to revere the other. But we have been misled in a number of ways: several factors help to explain the undue contrast between the careers of Wright and Hurston.

Richard Wright was a Black man born on a white, Mississippi plantation, and carried, by fits and starts, from one white, southern town to the next. In short, he was born into the antagonistic context of hostile whites wielding power against him. In this, his background mirrors our majority Black experience. And so, we readily accept the validity of *Native Son*'s Bigger Thomas, who pits himself against overwhelming, white force.

Moreover, *Native Son*, undoubtedly Wright's most influential book, conforms to white standards we have swallowed, regarding literary weight. It is apparently symbolic (rather than realistic), "serious" (unrelievedly grim), socio-political (rather than "personal") in its scale, and not so much "emotional" as impassioned in its deliberate execution.

Given the antagonistic premise of *Native Son*, the personal beginnings of Richard Wright, a Black man on enemy turf, it follows that his novel should pull you forward with its furious imagination, saturate the reader with varieties of hatred, and horror, climax in violence, and ram hard—ram hard—against a destiny of doom.

But suppose the premise is a different one?

Zora Neale Hurston was born and raised in an all-Black Florida town. In other words, she was born into a supportive, nourishing environment. And without exception, her work—as novelist, as anthropologist/diligent collector and preserver of Black folktale and myth—reflects this early and late, all-Black universe which was her actual and her creative world. You see her immovable, all-Black orientation in *Their Eyes Were Watching God*. Whites do not figure in this story of Black love; white anything or anybody is not important; what matters is the Black woman and the Black man who come together in a believable, contagious, full Black love that makes you want to go and seek and find, likewise, soon as you finish the book.

Since white America lies outside the Hurston universe, in fact as well as in her fiction, you do not run up on the man/the enemy; protest, narrowly conceived, is therefore beside the point; rhythm or tones of outrage or desperate flight would be wholly inappropriate in her text. Instead you slip into a total, Black reality where Black people do not represent issues; they represent their own, particular selves in a Family/Community setting that permits relaxation from hunted/warrior postures, and that fosters the natural, person postures of courting, jealousy, ambition, dream, sex, work, partying, sorrow, bitterness, celebration, and fellowship.

Unquestionably, *Their Eyes Were Watching God* is the prototypical Black novel of affirmation; it is the most successful, and convincing, and exemplary novel of Black love that we have, period. But the book gives us more: the story unrolls a fabulously written film of Black life freed from the constraints of oppression; here we may learn Black possibilities of ourselves if we could ever escape the hateful and alien context that has so deeply disturbed and mutilated our rightful efflorescence—*as people*. Consequently, this novel centers itself on Black love— even as *Native Son* rivets itself upon white hatred.

But, because Zora Neale Hurston was a woman, and because we have been misled into devaluating the functions of Black affirmation, her work has been derogated as romantic, the natural purview of a woman (i.e., unimportant), "personal" (not serious) in its scope, and assessed as *sui generis*, or idiosyncratic accomplishment of no lasting reverberation, or usefulness. All such derogation derives from ignorance and/or callow thinking we cannot afford to continue. Although few of us have known the happiness of an all-Black town/universe, every single one of us is the torn-away descendant of a completely Black/African world and, today, increasing numbers of us deem an all-Black circumstance/nation as our necessary, overriding goal. Accordingly, this Sister has given us the substance of an exceptional, but imperative vision, since her focus is both an historical truth and a contemporary aim. As for the derision of love as less important than war or violence, that is plain craziness, plain *white* craziness we do not need even to discuss.

And, is it true that *Native Son* represents you and me more than Hurston's heroine, Janie Starks? Both of them bespeak our hurt, our wished-for fulfillment, and, at various times, the nature and the level of our adjustment to complete fulfillment or, on the other hand, complete frustration. What's more, I do not accept that Wright and Hurston should be perceived, properly, as antipathetic in the wellsprings of their work. Bigger Thomas, the whole living and dying creation of him, teaches as much about the necessity of love, of being able to love without being destroyed, as Hurston's Janie Starks. Their address to this subject, this agonizingly central need, differs, perhaps, as men and women have been taught to cope with human existence differently. And, elsewhere, I submit that *Their Eyes* treats with a want and a hope and a tragic adjustment that is at least as reverberating, as universal—namely, positive (loving) self-fulfillment—as the material of *Native Son*, which emphasizes the negative trajectories of that same want, hope, and confrontation.

But, rightly, we should not choose between Bigger Thomas and Janie Starks; our lives are as big and as manifold and as pained and as happy as the two of them put together. We should equally value and equally emulate Black Protest and Black Affirmation, for we require both; one without the other is dangerous, and will leave us vulnerable to extinction of the body or the spirit. We owe thanks to both the struggle and the love: to the native sons among us, and to those whose eyes are watching their own gods.

11 On the Occasion of a Clear and Present Danger at Yale (1975)

In the spring of 1975, I became close friends with two remarkable Black students, Debbie and David Wright. This brother and sister team, their friends, a very few other members of Yale's faculty, and I formed an action group we called The Yale Attica Defense. In the middle of our organizing work to present a weekend program to inform and radicalize the Yale community vis-à-vis the issues of Attica, a program that would culminate with a benefit concert to raise defense monies, the Yale *Daily News* printed notice of an impending visit to campus by William Shockley. Shockley was enjoying much national exposure as an expert offering allegedly scientific justification for racist ideas such as the genetic inferiority of Black people and the consequently desirable sterilization of minority women. Perforce, our work on the Attica weekend came to a temporary halt. In the uproar pursuant to the news about Shockley, Yale's President and other like-minded officials stoutly defended the invitation to Shockley as proving institutional consecration to freedom of speech, along with related, spectacularly high-minded values.

On the afternoon immediately preceding the moment when Shockley was scheduled to give his talk, Yale's Black students convened a huge outdoor rally of protest. At this rally, I was asked to read my poetry, and to present a statement of position. It was hot and crowded. To me, the sight of several hundred students sprawled on the grass in front of the makeshift stage and microphones looked like the sixties, alive and well again. Accordingly, as I waited my turn, my mood was fairly buoyant.

One of my students, Theresa Johnson, a Black senior at Yale, came up to me. She peered into my sunglasses, awkwardly, for a moment. Then she said, "Why do they hate us, June? Why," she asked me, "why do they hate *me?*" I looked at the face of Theresa, at the tears on her face, and something inside me changed, irrevocably. I had conceptualized my statement as a written party to a malevolent but intellectual debate, but now I viewed it as part of a very dirty fight, which was, by its nature, apocalyptic: we could not afford to lose.

"On the Occasion of a Clear and Present Danger at Yale" is the statement I made at that rally. A lengthy excerpt was printed in the Yale *Daily News*.

One year later, I debated William Buckley on his TV program, *Firing Line*. Again, the ostensible issue was that of the First Amendment.

Some people have wondered: when the voice of a hatemonger-ing lunatic, when the thoughts of a man who well may be the harbinger of an American style Third Reich, shall be broadcast even among us, close by, less than several hours away, less than a thousand yards' distant from where we now stand, this after-noon, why do "they," the ones most likely to suffer, to be snuffed out, to be forcibly arrested from free being, free be-coming, a free, self-indicated destiny—why do "they" rally in a cultural display, a veritable festival of song and dance and music. What is the meaning of culture in the context of A Clear and Present Danger to the Ongoing Survival of Particular, Black, and Third World Lives?

In the first place, we do what we do because we do that: *we* exercise our prerogatives, *we* make the choices that we have made, for ourselves, whether anybody else understands or re-spects or likes it, or not.

In the second place, our cultural integrity, all that distinguishes us as "us," in this willfully polyglot America, is nothing less than the historic and the collective affirmation of our own self, today, in public and open visibility. It is our distinctive "us" culture, the beautiful, "get into it/down and up to go on and on" music of our beautiful, Black, and Third World, beleaguered, widely despised, stubbornly continuing lives. It is that music that we have eked out, devised, improvised, sanctified, and moved to, to keep our spirit intact, to bless and hold the spirit of us, as peoples, strong and holy as all life itself—life that we will not now, life that we have never, simply, or in any other way, let go.

But some still wonder, why, why this cultural display, this rally, as reaction to a clear and present danger? Why not debate the lunatic? Why not argue the man down?

In the first place, that would be a mistake. To accept, to adopt the terms of the man, to meet the man on his terms, his schedule, and in his fashion, to accommodate your enemy by accepting anything whatever that issues from him, and his kind, is an obvious mistake that we do not need to contemplate.

In the second place, what is the ostensible crux of the debate some would have us engage in with our enemy? Yale will tell you that the crux of the matter is freedom of speech. This is a joke. This is an insult to injury. There has never been and there will never be absolute freedom of speech in this country. If I say something interpreted as "conspiring against," or if I say something interpreted as "incitement to riot," then, according to American law, I lose the right to say those things. My freedom of speech clearly breaks down where the self-preserving interests of the state, the self-preserving interests of property, are concerned. Moreover, if Yale, if any institution, nevertheless, insists upon providing me with a forum for my "conspiring" and/or "incitement to riot," then Yale, then any such institution is an accessory to my crime—the crime of speech that constitutes a clear and present danger to the self-preserving interests of some other person, or group, or lawful entity. I say that Yale University, by knowingly providing a forum for the presentation of ideas that clearly threaten the self-preservation of people— living Black people/Third World people, as well as Black and Third World peoples yet unborn—I say that Yale University, by so doing, is *not* some kind of a "bastion of free speech": it is, rather, an accessory to the crime such speech represents; it is an accessory to the crime of creating a clear and present danger to the lives and the possible lives such willful speech denigrates, and condemns to death.

But what is this sudden rush to the cause of freedom? Where is the evidence of Yale University's commitment to freedom? What freedom does this institution care about? Is it the freedom to maintain traditions based upon hundreds of years of genocide, theft, rape, humiliation, and hypocrisy? Is it the freedom to project a respectability for the forces of conservatism: social, political, academic conservatism: the conservation of bloody, terrifying, life-denying, arrogant traditions of a self-appointed elite of the world? Is it the freedom to serve the status quo, the unearned privileges of unearned/stolen wealth, the preferential meanings of the accidents of class and color, the perspectives, the policies, and the killer practices of the CIA/FBI/US Armed Forces/General Motors/Esso/Gulf/Bank of America status quo? Show me the freedom that this University upholds: show it to me in its admission policies. Show it to me in its financial aid programs. Show it to me in its curriculum, in its required readings, in the color, the sex, the viewpoints of its faculty. Show me this freedom that this institution holds dear.

As I said, the crux of the matter is not Freedom of Speech. That is the misbegotten propaganda propagated by our enemies. The crux of the matter, the clear and present danger to our very lives, points to a far more fundamental issue. It is the issue of life against death. "We hold these truths to be self-evident, that all men are created equal and endowed with certain inalienable rights, among them life—" LIFE, Life: the freedom to live, the freedom to stay alive, the freedom to make life, the freedom to bring new life into and among our lives, the freedom to choose and possess life and again life. Next to that fundamental freedom, the freedom to be alive and to perpetuate our own lives, what is something called Freedom of Speech?

So we will not debate a lunatic who dares to dispute the validity, the value of Black and Third World and/or any other human life. Our lives are not debatable. We are, we have survived, we will be as we will choose for ourselves. We will continue to struggle for our survival and for the freedom of our children who will survive us by every means we choose to use. That much is clear.

But, if we are not debatable, and we are *not* debatable, we are, however, vulnerable. We can be killed. We can be sterilized. We can be kept out, pushed down, starved, shot, gassed, lynched, stunted, warped, and eliminated, altogether, from liberty, from our own pursuit of our own happiness. It's happened before. It's happening now.

Right now, in America, we, Black people, Third World peoples, poor people, in general, are being sterilized: homogenized into nonexistence, sterilized: made incapable of bearing children, sterilized: lobotomized into cooperative, peaceable, vegetable remnants, sterilized: punished for having a man in the house, a father, a lover, and punished for having babies. Children are reasons, right now, why the Black and Third World and poor peoples of America must suffer punishments even of starvation, illness, shockingly inadequate shelter, and death.

Right now, in America, the depression is wasting away the will to live and the life resources of the increasing poor of America who face only an unrelieved, ever-worsening subjugation by poverty, by hunger, by calculated doom.

Right now, and right here, the poor and the Black and the Third World peoples here, at Yale, must testify to repeated and growing prospects of private and state-supported policies to destroy and extirpate "us" from this diseased body politic of these United States. We are vulnerable, yes, but debatable, no. And I ask you: What will happen after this rally, after this cultural display? Will you rally in another form, 365 days of every coming year, go to the meetings, seek out the issues, monitor activities ("crackpot" as well as "traditional"), forge helpful ties of real service to our brothers and sisters in New Haven, in the rest of America, in Africa, and Asia, foster and support every event that will raise consciousness, and money, on behalf of ourselves and the other, multimillion targets and victims of the American status quo?

94

Will you assume responsibility for your life, in these many, urgent ways, will you assume responsibility for your life, and my life, and our lives, the lives that are now, and that have always been, endangered and attacked by our enemies operating under deliberately misleading, asinine slogans such as the misapplied slogan of Freedom of Speech?

With all my heart, I hope so.

12 Notes of a Barnard Dropout (1975)

In 1975, Alice Walker and I jointly received The Reid
Lectureship at Barnard College, an honor we were pleased to
share. I presented these *Notes of a Barnard Dropout* in dialog
with Alice, at Lehman Auditorium, Barnard College, November
11, 1975. Our papers were then released as a small booklet
published by the Women's Center at Barnard.

Let me try, today, to share with you my perspective on things,
and let me offer a few ideas about how, and why, I came to it.
You could probably characterize my worldview as apocalyptic
—or, let's just say that I believe that, as Aretha sings the song,
A CHANGE IS GONNA COME.

To be honest, I expect apocalypse, or I look for and I work
for defeat of international evil, indifference, and suffering, only
when I am not otherwise stunned by the odds, temporarily
paralyzed by revulsion and grieving despair.

But life itself compels an optimism. It does not seem reasonable that the majority of the peoples of the world should,
finally, lose on possibilities of dignified existence, joy, and rational justice as a global experiment to be pursued and fiercely
protected. It seems unreasonable that more than 400 million
people, right now, must struggle against hunger and starvation,
even while there is arable earth aplenty to feed and nourish
every one of us. It does not seem reasonable that the color of

your skin should curse and condemn all of your days and the days of your children. It seems preposterous that gender, that being a woman, anywhere in the world, should elicit contempt, or fear, or ridicule, and serious deprivation of rights to be, to become, to embrace whatever you choose.

And, here, in this country, it seems absurd that we should knuckle to a leadership of lies, treachery, misbegotten self-righteousness, wanton butchery committed in our name, our national self-interest, and a brutal, stupid willingness to define issues, first and finally, in terms of money—not human life, but money. This seems to me an implicitly untenable state of affairs.

I cannot accept that "balance the budget" will ultimately eclipse a concern to balance the distribution and availability of wealth, of chances for self-respecting survival.

It seems to me merely reasonable, for instance, that the mayor of the City of New York should instigate a tax strike against Washington, and call upon private employers to follow suit. Since this city gives 19 billion dollars to the Feds, and receives, in return, a maximum of 8 billion dollars back regardless of how you compute things, and since the impending default of New York will mean a colossal loss of livelihood, and a loss of services to keep life feasible in the city—for human life, I mean —and since the federal government is manifestly uninterested in serving these people it is bold to represent, or, at least, to deny, then it seems merely reasonable to withhold our moneys, 19 billions of dollars of the peoples of New York, to use those funds for the emergency human life needs of our city. A tax strike will remind Washington that taxation without representation of the interests of those so burdened has never been a popular idea.

Now I have given you some of the contents of my optimism, or worldview.

When I try to understand why or how I arrived where I am, one image keeps recurring. At nights, in Brooklyn, in our home, I would sit, studying, or eating in the kitchen, as my mother, her progress a slow and heavy tread on the wooden stairs, came up from the basement, carrying heavy pails of ashes from the furnace. This ritual nightmare never ended; even after a stroke, my mother carried the ashes up from the basement furnace, her breathing short and ragged, her thin frame crooked and lopsided from the weight of those filthy pails. Carrying the ashes up, and outside, you see, was her responsibility, as my father defined things. What would you have him do? Stay home from work to empty the ashes? Or switch to a day shift, which would mean less money, a few dollars less even, than he earned by working nights? These were rhetorical questions only. The ashes remained the responsibility of my mother, who, I must add, also worked, whenever her health allowed, as a private duty nurse, also at night. Later, she worked the so-called midnight shift. Why? Because nighttime was, otherwise, incredibly barren for her, with my father away, and because nighttime duty meant a little more money for the family. Throughout my growing up, my parents worked as hard as they could devise, and yet we never had a car, my parents never had a vacation, our family never knew what it was to feel satisfied, or proud, or basically secure. In fact, more than anything else, my father felt himself a man despised, a man whose maximal efforts to achieve would be regarded by the powerful as pitiful, as ridiculous. He suffered for this, and he made my mother suffer for this.

Well, I was born in Harlem, and raised in Bedford-Stuyvesant. Then, when I was twelve or thirteen, I was sent away to prep school. In other words, I began my life in a completely Black universe, and then for the three years of prep school, found myself completely immersed in a white universe. When I came to Barnard, what I hoped to find, therefore, was a connection; I hoped that Barnard College—which I attended while living at home, in Brooklyn—I hoped that Barnard College would either give me the connection between the apparently unrelated worlds of white and Black, or that this college would enable me to make that connection for myself.

Let me say, at once, that whereas Barnard, or in other words, a relatively conventional, elitist education, gave me friends (and one of them introduced me to architecture as environmental control); whereas Barnard gave me the father of my son (that is also to say that Columbia College was, even in 1954, right across the street); whereas Barnard trained me to think independently, honed my capacity for ingestion of materials, forced me to master analytical skills, and taught me the difference between an Ionian and a Corinthian column; whereas Barnard College changed me in these various respects, not listed according to importance, please note, it did not, none of the courses of study, nothing about the teaching, made the connection for me, or facilitated my discovery of a connection.

After school, every day, I went home via the subway. That was the only connection I encountered: a dirty, alive, underground trip between the Parthenon and what was subsequently termed the ghetto.

It was quite a ride. But, at Barnard, there was one great teacher whom I was privileged to know, Barry Ulanov. And in freshman English I remember to this day two assignments for which I will always feel gratitude. One was the assignment of a paper to pull together, I think he said "somehow," Alfred North Whitehead's *Aims of Education* and Edith Hamilton's *Mythology*. Many of my classmates became more or less suicidal as they reflected on this task. But I thought, damn, if you can synthesize Whitehead with Greek mythology, then maybe you can bring the Parthenon to Bedford-Stuyvesant, and make it *all* real.

The other assignment Barry Ulanov gave to us came in the form of a surprise, in-class exam: write about anything you want, without using any forms of the verbs *to be* and *to have*. That's extremely difficult, in case you don't know. And I learned more about the functions of our concepts of Being and Having, from that fifty minutes of class, than I had ever known, or considered, until that moment, altogether.

On the debit side of things, the farce side of Barnard, I must mention a required zoology lab. You had to take three hours of lab. That was in addition to three hours of standing room only lectures in zoology, held in the Minor Latham Playhouse. But the lab was amazing; every experiment was rigged. It turned out there were predetermined right answers and wrong answers. I mean, they gave you these ears of corn, see, and you were supposed to count the blue kernels, the white kernels, the red kernels, and the yellow. Can you imagine a more weird way to spend time? If you came up with too many blues, or reds, you were wrong. I couldn't believe it. What kind of a rigged, pro forma, nonexperiment was this? Counting corn kernels that had already, long ago, been counted, and summed up into some kind of an unassailable genetic principle? Pure farce.

But to return to the credit side. The one year of sociology that I took was helpful even though the woman teaching the course on the family, or marriage, used to show up in dark glasses that failed to conceal her black eyes (and she seemed to have a black eye, at least one black eye, throughout the semester). Even so, I remember Professor Samuel Barber telling us that, if you really assimilated the perspectives and assumptions of that discipline, you could never be bored. He was telling the truth. Sociology even helped me to get through a lot of classes that, pre-sociology, I would have cut, without thinking twice about it. Plus, it gave me a new way to think about everything.

But nothing at Barnard, and no one at Barnard, ever, once, formulated, and expressed, the necessity, the political necessity, if you will, for the knowledge they required you to absorb. Precedent and tradition, after all, are not of themselves sufficient justification for anything whatever. And nobody, and not a single course of study at Barnard, ever spoke to issues judged critical, or to possible commitments evaluated as urgent. More specifically, no one ever presented me with a single Black author, poet, historian, personage, or idea, for that matter. Nor was I ever assigned a single woman to study as a thinker, or writer, or poet, or life force. Nothing that I learned, here, lessened my feeling of pain and confusion and bitterness as related to my origins: my street, my family, my friends. Nothing showed me how I might try to alter the political and economic realities underlying our Black condition in white America.

Nothing that I learned here prepared me for not being able to get a taxi, anywhere, when I can afford one. Nothing that I learned here prepared me for the tragedy of the death of the Black boy that produced the Harlem Riot of 1964, nor the atrocious, nonreporting by white media, of what actually happened. Nothing, here, prepared me for the travesty of high-paid, "anti-

100

poverty" planning and research on the lower East Side, research that yielded no new, safe housing to the peoples forced to live there, in continuous jeopardy. And so forth.

And because Barnard College did not teach me necessity, nor prime my awareness as to urgencies of need around the world, nor galvanize my heart around the critical nature of conflicts between the powerful and the powerless, and, because, beyond everything else, it was not going to be school, evidently, but life-after-school, that would teach me the necessities for radical change, and revolution, I left. I dropped out of Barnard. It was, apparently, an optional experience.

And so I continue: a Black woman who would be an agent for change, an active member of the hoped-for apocalypse. I am somebody seeking to make, or to create, revolutionary connections between the full identity of my love, of what hurts me, or fills me with nausea, and the way things are: what we are forced to learn, to "master," what we are trained to ignore, what we are bribed into accepting, what we are rewarded for doing, or not doing...

Ah, Momma,
Did the house ever know the nighttime of your spirit, the flash and flame of you who, once, when we crouched in what you called "the little room," where your dresses hung in their pallid colorings—an uninteresting row of uniforms—and where there were dusty, sweet-smelling boxes of costume jewelry that, nevertheless, shone like rubies, gold, and diamonds, once, in that place where the secondhand mirror blurred the person, dull, that place without windows, with doors instead of walls, so that your small-space most resembled a large and rather haphazard closet, once, in there, you told me, whispering, that once, you wanted to become an artist: someone, you explained, who could just boldly go and sit near the top of a hill, and watch the setting of the sun

Ah, Momma!
You said this had been your wish when you were quite as young as I was then, a twelve- or thirteen-year-old girl who heard

your confidence with almost terrified amazement. What had happened to you, and your wish?

Ah, Momma:
"The little room"—of your secrets, your costumery, perfumes, and photographs of an old boyfriend you never married (for reasons not truly clear to me because I saw you make sure, time after time, that his pictures were being kept as clean and as safely as possible)—the "little room" adjoined the kitchen, the kitchen where no mystery survived, except for the mystery of you: woman who covered her thick, and long, black hair with a starched, white nurse's cap when she went "on duty" away from our home, into the hospital I came to hate, jealously, woman who rolled up her wild and heavy, beautiful hair before she went to bed, woman who tied a headrag around the waving, well-washed braids, or lengthy fat curls of her hair, while she moved, without particular grace, between the table and the stove, between the sink and the table, around and around in the ugly, spacious kitchen where you never dreamed about what you might do instead, and where you taught me to set down silverware, and even fresh-cut flowers from the garden, without appetite, without expectation

It was not there, in that open, square cookery where you spent most of the days, it was not there, where nothing ever tasted sweet or sharp enough to sate the yearnings I began to suspect inside your eyes, and also inside the eyes of my father, it was not there that I began to hunger for the sun as my own, legitimate preoccupation; it was not there, in the kitchen, that I began, really, to love you

Ah, Momma,
It was where I found you, hidden away, in your "little room," where your life, the rhythms of your sacrifice, the ritual of your bowed head, and your laughter, always partly concealed, where all of you, womanly, reverberated big as the whole house, it was there that I came, humbly, into an angry, an absolute determination that I would, one day, prove myself to be, in fact, your daughter
Ah, Momma, I am still trying

13 Angola: A Victory and a Promise (1976)

There are few books that make my hands tremble whenever I take them down from the shelves, to read. One of these is *Sacred Hope*, by Agostinho Neto, first President of The People's Republic of Angola.

Neto is now dead. And the lover from Mississippi who gave these poems to me is no longer my comrade and my friend. But Agostinho Neto, his poetry and his life as a poet continue to chasten and to challenge my own.

This essay was written in the summer of 1976 and later published in *First World* where I appended a list of organizations to which readers might apply for the purpose of actively joining the liberation struggles in Southern Africa.

That we as African people are different, that the difference is worth cherishing, and beautiful, that we are capable of fighting and of triumph: these concepts about ourselves enjoyed even popular currency toward the end of the sixties, here in the United States. But the crumbling of morale, the assassination of leaders, the systematic disintegration of our meager gains from that era have left us, today, with apparently small belief, no summoning voice, and ever yet worsening needs. Were these concepts merely self-flattering constructions of a desperately collective mind? In this real world, can we validate an imagery of our survival that we would want our children to embrace, as the truth?

However difficult these questions may be to answer, in the context of this country, and in the privacy of our own hearts, there is a tumult, a leavening, a transforming, redoubtable, cataclysmic, new history of African peoples unrolling in Africa. It is a process, a momentum certain to intersect with our strangely Afro-American lives, in a decisive way, before we reach the 1980s. I refer, of course, to the impending total liberation of Southern Africa, by the African peoples living there, and their proven allies.

Clearly we may derive the most serious kind of inspiration from the ongoing struggle of our African Brothers and Sisters who remain undaunted despite massacre, hunger, technological "odds," and the grievous loss of lives, year after year of unremitting, lethal, and unspeakably arrogant, oppression. They continue to win, battling to be free, and to start the world over again, according to their own dreams and values.

It also seems clear that we may rightfully claim validation for our self-respecting self-imagery to the exact degree that we devise activist, and disinterested, means of alliance with those peoples of Southern Africa for whom the terrors of war loom close, either immediately behind or ahead of them.

Without question, there is much that we can do to aid and expedite the African liberation of all of Southern Africa. And, if there is any doubt as to the potential influence of an organized American minority, one minute's reflection on the manifest power of the Israeli lobby in Washington should wipe that out.

But even Southern Africa is more immense and diversified than we can easily imagine. To gain some definite sense and feeling about the peoples involved, perhaps it would be helpful to look closely at the single nation state of the People's Republic of Angola, where a stunning triumph of self-determination has recently been achieved. Nine times larger than New York State, or three times the size of California, with a population of approximately six million, the People's Republic of Angola has been deemed potentially the wealthiest nation of Africa; enormous deposits of copper, iron, diamonds, manganese, titanium, and oil exist inside its boundaries. In addition, vast timber resources and a coffee-producing capacity that would rank its harvest third or fourth in the world augur very well for the continuing self-sufficiency of the Angolans. It is furthermore conceivable that the potential agricultural output of the People's Republic of Angola could soon function as an important bread-basket resource for the entire continent. We are talking, then, of a victory with spectacular implications for continental, as well as diaspora, Africans, everywhere.

Angolan resistance to the Portuguese dates back as far as the seventeenth century when Rainha Jinga, a ruling queen of that period, mobilized her people and, for a while, successfully blocked colonial encroachment. In our time, resistance and even-tual revolution have been clasped as the central life purpose of Angolan men and women distinguished by devout perse-verance, quite regardless of the degree, or length, of the perse-cution inflicted upon them. For example, the MPLA (the Popular Movement for the Liberation of Angola) was founded twenty years ago, in December 1956. The struggle has taken two dec-ades to reach the fruition we can now celebrate and help to secure. Throughout, "poetry was not simply a substitute for political struggle. It was intrinsic to that struggle. The cultural assimilation of the intellectual, at one pole, and the denial of culture to the masses of the people, at the other, demanded that the revolutionary intellectual, basing himself on the bitter material reality of the life of the people, express the emotional essence of his identification with the people, of the explosion lying beneath the surface of the colonial condition, and of the future already visible in the decay of the present . . . Poetry, more than any other literary form, is capable of expressing collective emotion." [1]

One of the Angolan poet revolutionaries, Antonio Jacinto, has written a poem I find astonishing in its impassioned beauty and obvious love. Jacinto, imprisoned for fourteen years by the Portuguese, has managed to imprint his anguish not only re-sulting from his forced separation from his beloved, he has also expressed, with powerful tenderness, the anguish felt by the

---

[1] *Sacred Hope* by Agostinho Neto, from the Introduction by Marga Holness p. xxi (Nairobi, Kenya, East Africa Publishing House, 1972).

revolutionary intellectual who is estranged from his people by
the illiteracy imposed on them, under colonial rule.

LETTER FROM A CONTRACT WORKER

I wanted to write you a letter
my love
a letter to tell
of this longing
to see you
and this fear
of losing you
of this thing which deeper than I want, I feel
a nameless pain which pursues me
a sorrow wrapped about my life.

I wanted to write you a letter
my love
a letter of intimate secrets
a letter of memories of you
of you
your lips as red as the tcula fruit
your hair black as the dark diloa fish
your eyes gentle as the macongue
your breasts hard as young maboque fruit
your light walk
your caresses
better than any that I find down here.

I wanted to write you a letter
my love
to bring back our days together in our
                    secret haunts
nights lost in the long grass
to bring back the shadow of your legs
and the moonlight filtering through the
          endless palms,

to bring back the madness of our passion
and the bitterness of separation.

I wanted to write you a letter
my love
which you could not read without crying
which you would hide from your father Bombo
and conceal from your mother Kieza
which you would read without the indifference
of forgetfulness,
a letter which would make any other
in all Kilombo worthless.

I wanted to write you a letter
my love
a letter which the passing wind would take
a letter which the cashew and the coffee trees,
the hyenas and the buffalo,
the cymens and the river fish
could hear
the plants and the animals
pitying our sharp sorrow
from song to song
lament to lament
breath to caught breath
would leave to you, pure and hot,
the burning
the sorrowful words of the letter
I wanted to write you

I wanted to write you a letter
But my love, I don't know why it is,
why, why, why it is, my love,
but you can't read
and I—oh the hopelessness—I can't write.

   The victory of the spirit of Jacinto, as evinced in his poem,
suggests the fullness of the revolution being enacted within

the People's Republic of Angola. Beyond the decisive expulsion of their enemies, the reconstruction of their country in the light of full liberation priorities has led, for instance, to the appointment of Angolan women to some of the highest governmental responsibilities. Maria Da Assuncao Vahekeny is Secretary for Social Affairs, and Olga Lima is the Director of Political Affairs for the Ministry of Foreign Affairs, just to cite two instances of the revised status of women, which became a critical aspect of the revolution when Angolan women shouldered their rifles and went to war, side by side with Angolan men.

At the head of the Angolan revolution, which is now in its postwar, reconstruction stage, stands President Agostinho Neto, a foremost Angolan poet and physician. Born September 17, 1922, in a small village about 60 kilometers from Luanda, Neto's first book of poems was published in 1955 while he was under political arrest for the second time, in Portugal. In 1958, he qualified as a doctor and married Maria Eugenia on the day of his graduation. Increasingly engaged in the liberation efforts of his people in Angola, Neto was imprisoned, and exiled, intermittently from this date forward. In 1960, he was arrested in the examining room of his office in Luanda, and a peaceful protest by the people of his birthplace, the village of Icolo e Bengo, provoked the Portuguese massacre of thirty unarmed men, women, and children.

From this point, Portuguese attempts to exterminate all Angolan liberation movements assumed ever more barbarous form, even as the Angolan revolutionaries systematically extended the breadth of the peoples they represented and recruited into the war. Neto was made Honorary President of the MPLA directly following his 1960 imprisonment, and international campaigns to save his life and to protect him from torture were launched around the world. By 1961, his poems had been anthologized in several places and they were fast becoming available to a growing readership in seven languages. Neto became the symbol, the rallying focus, as well as the individual reality of oppressed Angola determined to survive, with freedom.

By 1975, Portugal was constrained to negotiate an agreement to independence. All the liberation movements of African Angola signed this document and, one month afterward, in February 1975, a fierce battle ensued among these contending groups—the FNLA, UNITA, and the MPLA. But, despite American and South African covert and overt interference in the intra-Angolan battling, the MPLA emerged the unarguable victor and ruling political administration, in February of the next year. Although the United States still withholds official recognition of the People's Republic of Angola, as of this writing, 28 African states now recognize this government, and the People's Republic of Angola was admitted to the O.A.U. (Organization of African Unity) as its 47th member, February 1976.

In his foreword to *Sacred Hope*, the first volume of Agostinho Neto's poetry to become accessible to us, his long-term friend and admirer, Basil Davidson, writes: "He is loved or he is feared as the spokesman of a people fighting to be free. He is followed or opposed as the leader of a struggle that all men must fight in their different times and places, and all women too, shaking off the past, transforming the present. The poet is all these things, and with a purity of aim and courage that are inseparable from the man that he was and the man he has become. But he is also a poet, ineluctably a poet, inescapably a poet; and it's in his poetry, as in the poetry of others of his kind, that you may come upon the keys to all the rest."

Here are three poems by Agostinho Neto, poet and President of the People's Republic of Angola:

KINAXIX

I liked to sit
on a bench at kinaxixi
at six o'clock of a very hot evening
and stay there . . .

Someone would come
perhaps to sit
to sit beside me

And I would see the black faces of people
going up the alleyway
leisurely
expressing absence in the hybrid Kimbundo
of their talk

I would see the weary steps
of serfs whose parents were also serfs
seeking here love there glory
beyond drunkenness in every alcohol

Neither happiness nor hate

When the sun went down
they would light the lamps
and I
would go off aimlessly
thinking that our life is simple after all
too simple
for he who is tired and has to walk on.

WESTERN CIVILIZATION

Sheets of tin nailed to posts
driven in the ground
make up the house.

Some rags complete
the intimate landscape.

The sun slanting through cracks
welcomes the owner

After twelve hours of slave
labour.

breaking rock
shifting rock

breaking rock
shifting rock
fair weather
wet weather
breaking rock
shifting rock

Old age comes early

a mat on dark nights
is enough when he dies
gratefully
of hunger.

CREATE

Create create
create in mind create in muscle create in nerve
create in man create in the masses
create
create with dry eyes

create create
over the profanation of the forest
over the brazen fortress of the whip
create over the perfume of sawn trunks
create
create with dry eyes

create create
bursts of laughter over the derision of the *palmatoria*

courage in the tips of the planter's boots
strength in the splintering of battered-in doors
firmness in the red blood of insecurity
create
create with dry eyes

create create
stars over the warrior's sledge-hammer
peace over children's weeping
peace over sweat over the tears of contract labour
peace over hatred
create
create peace with dry eyes

create create
create freedom in the slave stars
manacles of love on the paganised paths of love
festive sounds over swinging bodies on simulated gallows

create
create love with dry eyes.

THREE

14 Declaration of an Independence I Would Just as Soon Not Have (1976)

If it is not apparent from the text, then let me make it clear that I wrote this from the inside. As a Black woman, and as a human being within the First World Movement, and as a woman who loves women as well as she loves men. *Ms.* magazine published this essay under their title, "Second Thoughts of a Black Feminist." My question at the end of this piece was answered by Black women who wrote to me, care of *Ms.*, from all over the country. Yes, they said, you are not alone!

I know I am not alone. There must be hundreds of other women, maybe thousands, who feel as I do. There may be hundreds of men who want the same drastic things to happen. But how do you hook up with them? How can you interlink your own struggle and goals with these myriad, hypothetical people who are hidden entirely or else concealed by stereotype and/or generalities of "platform" such as any movement seems to spawn? I don't know. And I don't like it, this being alone when it is clear that there will have to be multitudes working together, around the world, if radical and positive change can be forced upon the heinous status quo I despise in all its overwhelming power.

For example, suppose the hunger and the famine afflicting some 800 million lives on earth is a fact that leaves you nauseous, jumpy, and chronically enraged. No matter how intense your wrath may be, no matter how personally knowledgeable you may be about the cause and the conceivable remedies for this monstrous and unnecessary curse upon innocent human beings, you, by yourself, can do damned little, if anything, to destroy these facts of abject experience. But what can you join? Where can you sign up, sign in?

Or suppose you consider children, as I do, the only blameless people alive. And suppose you possess all the eyeball evidence, all the statistics, that indicate a majority of Black youngsters doomed to semi-illiteracy and/or obsolete vocational training for jobs, livelihoods, that disappeared from the real life marketplace at least five years ago. Or suppose you love children and you cannot forget that there are entire countries, even in this same hemisphere, where four- and five-year-olds, where nine- and ten-year-olds, have been abandoned, kicked out of their homes, or worse, where so-called packs of these little people must scavenge the garbage cans and the very streets for something to eat before they finally lie down to sleep in gutters and doorways, under the soiled newspapers that consistently fail to report the degrading fact that the children will probably not survive. What do you do? Where are the hands you can clasp in dedication against such enormous reasons for shame?

Or what about the poor, the dispossessed, families of America? Once you realize that Welfare supports have steadily declined, for instance, in the face of unprecedented, inflationary increases in the cost of living, once you understand what this particular disequilibrium implies for a family of five children and their mother who must, nevertheless, manage to secure food, heat, warm enough clothing, carfare, moneys for medical care, and the rent, where can you turn, effectively, to end this death-dealing disgrace? If you happen to be a Black woman, as I am, and a so-called female head of household, then, in an unlimited number of ways, you undoubtedly recognize that you are simply another unacknowledged single mother represented solely by official figures that bespeak a relentlessly rising percentage of Black people, per se: you are damned as Black, damned as a woman, and damned as a quote female head of household unquote. Can you point me toward the movement directly addressing the special, inexorable hardships borne by me and my sisters in like, involuntary circumstances?

Well, for a long time I thought it was perfectly fine to be alone, as far as political cause was concerned. You wrote poems, free-lance exposé articles, essays proposing remedies, even novels demonstrating the feasibility of solutions that you ardently trusted as possibilities for activist commitment. Or you hitched onto ad hoc committees against this or that nightmare and, when and if you had the bucks, you made tax-deductible donations of endorsement for whatever public fight seemed to you among the most urgent to be won. What did this yield? I felt pretty good, yes, and comfortable with my conscience. But nothing changed, nothing ever really changed as the result of such loner activity.

So now I am no longer as silly, as vaingloriously innocent, as I was. It is plainly the truth that, whatever its vast and various dimensions, human misery is the predicted, aforethought consequence of deliberate, deliberated arrangements of power that would distort the whole planet into miserly, personal rights of property belonging to extremely few men and their egotistical and/or avaricious interests. Ad hoc, loner protests will not make the difference, will not impose the revolutionary changes such undue suffering demands. I think it is necessary to form or join a well-defined organization that can and will work to destroy the status quo as ruthlessly, as zealously, as nonstop in its momentum, as are the enemy forces surely arrayed against our goals. Accordingly, since the bloody close of the Civil Rights era I have sought, repeatedly, just such a body of intelligently inclusive feelings and aims. I have found that there are three movements that compel my willing respect and hopes. But I have also learned that there exists, in each of these movements, a ranking of priorities, a peculiarity of perspective, that conflicts with the other two, in an apparently irreconcilable manner. Furthermore, since every one of these movements calls for liberation of some kind, it has become necessary to try and define what liberation apparently signifies to the Black Movement, the Third World Movement, and the Women's Movement, respectively. In this effort, I have encountered a woeful magnitude of internecine, unfortunate, and basically untenable conflicts of analysis. Let me break down what I mean, exactly: 1. The Black Movement: This is the battle I have attempted to help define, and forward, as though my own life depended on its success. In truth, my life does depend on the outcome of our Black struggles for freedom to be ourselves, in self-respecting self-sufficiency. But where can you find serious Black spokesmen, or women, for the impoverished, hungry, state-dependent Black peoples among us who still amount to more than a third of our total population? And why does it continue to be the case that, when our ostensible leadership talks about the "liberation of the Black man" that is precisely, and only, what they mean? How is it even imaginable that Black men would presume to formulate the Black Movement and the Women's movement as either/or, antithetical alternatives of focus? As a Black woman, I view such a formulation with a mixture of incredulity and grief: The irreducible majority of Black people continues to be composed of Black women. And, whereas many Black sons and daughters have never known our Black fathers, or a nurturing, supportive Black man in our daily lives, all Black people have most certainly been raised, and cared for, by Black women: mothers, grandmothers, aunts. In addition, and despite the prevalent bullshit to the contrary, Black women continue to occupy the absolutely lowest rungs of the labor force in the United States, we continue to receive the lowest pay of any group of workers, and we endure the highest rate of unemployment. If that status does not cry out for liberation, specifically as Black women, then I am hopelessly out of touch with my own pre-ordained reality.

On another front, I have difficulty comprehending our alleged Black leaders who postulate an antithetical relationship between the destinies of Afro-Americans and the fate of the First World —which is too commonly, and mistakenly, termed the "Third World." I cannot understand how we, Afro-Americans, have contended with racism, with life-denying exploitation, with brute-powerful despising of our culture, our languages, our gods, our children—how we have grappled with such a bedeviled history for more than four centuries and yet, today, cannot grasp the identical stakes, the identical sources of evil and oppression, that obtain in the lives of our First World brothers and sisters. Moreover, I cannot understand how any of us can fail to perceive the necessarily international nature of our oppression and, hence, our need for international unity and planned rebellion. 2. The First World Movements: The multimillion-fold majority of the peoples on earth are neither white, nor powerful, nor exempt from terrifying syndromes of disease, hunger, poverty that defies description, and prospects for worse privation or demeaning subsistence. With all my heart and mind I would strive in any way I could to eradicate the origins of such colossal exploitation and abuse. But, except for the inspired exceptions of China, Cuba, and Tanzania, it appears that class divisions still suffocate the clearly legitimate aspirations of most First World Peoples, and that the status enjoined upon women is that of a serf, at best. Consequently, one can contribute to African liberation campaigns or to anti-famine collectives, yes, but one must also wrestle with sober misgivings. Will these funds reach the afflicted peoples of your concern, or will the dollar bills merely fill the pockets of neo-colonial bourgeoisie who travel through the countryside in Mercedes-Benz limousines, air-conditioned and bullet-proofed against the men and women they have been empowered to serve? And how will the eventual victory be celebrated? Will the women cook the feast and then fear to share it with their menfolk at the same table, at the same time, on a basis of mutual regard and cherishing? What will victory mean for the traditional outcasts, the traditional lowest of the low: the poor, and women, generally? Will the changing of the color of the guards bring about a verifiable change of policy and objectives? Do we have to expect that formerly colonized, newly independent, nation states will mistakenly pursue paths that verily imitate the powers that enslaved them? Will none of the newly emerging leaders reject, for example, industrialization and their ongoing dependence upon outside, hostile corporations and military allies, and concentrate, instead, upon land reform and intensive agrarian development that will determine the actuality of their independence?

3. The Women's Movement: I remain determined to fight for equal rights of fulfillment and exploration, as a person who is female. And for a while, and with exhilaration, I immersed myself in primer readings about the nature of women's subjugation, and about the legislative and social and economic proposals for corrective action. But then I began to falter in my excitement, in my sense of overdue confirmation, and sisterhood. The Women's Movement did not seem as large, in its avowed concerns, or as complicated, as I believe the world is large and complicated. Exceedingly little attention was granted to the problems of working class or poor people, to the victimization of Black women who head families, by themselves. Nowhere did I see an espousal of the struggles to end the predicament of children everywhere—a cause that seemed natural to me, as a woman. Nor did I detect a feeling awareness that you cannot aid half a people; you have to seek to assist the men as well as the women of any oppressed group. Nor have I discovered a political breadth of response that would certainly include, for example, the C.I.A. murder of Patrice Lumumba, Martin Luther King, Jr., and President Allende of Chile, in a disastrous triumph of imperialistic will.

Finally, there is the question of the liberation of women. Will we liberate ourselves so that the caring for children, the teaching, the loving, healing, person-oriented values that have always distinguished us will be revered and honored at least commensurate to the honors accorded bank managers, lieutenant colonels, and the executive corporate elite? Or will we liberate ourselves so that we can militantly abandon those attributes and functions, so that we can despise our own warmth and generosity even as men have done, for ages?

And if women loving other women and/or women in love with women will be part and parcel of the manifest revolution we want to win, does that mean that we should condone lecherous, exploitative, shallow, acting out, and pathological behavior by women who term themselves lesbians—in much the same way that we, Black people, once voluntarily called ourselves *niggas* out of a convoluted mood of defiance, a mood that proved to be heavily penetrated by unconscious, continuing self-hatred?

That is behavior, after all, that is the use of, that is submission to, an enemy concept such as we would never condone, or welcome, in interracial or heterosexual relationships of any sort.

I would hope that the sum total of the liberation struggles I have attempted to sketch, and briefly criticize, would mean this: That I will be free to be who I am, Black and female, without fear, without pain, without humiliation. That I will be free to become whatever my life requires of me, without posturing, without compromise, without terror. That I will soon be able, realistically, to assume the dignified fulfillment of the dreams and needs and potentialities of most of the men, women, and children alive, today. That I can count upon a sisterhood and a brotherhood that will let me give my life to its consecration, without equivocating, without sorrow. That my son, who is a Black man, and that I, a Black woman, may keep faith with each other, and with those others whom we may have the privilege to serve, and to join.

Toward these ends, I have written this account of one woman's declaration of an independence I would just as soon not have I believe I am not alone. Please verify

15 Thinking about My Poetry (1977)

Things That I Do in the Dark, my selected poems spanning twenty years, was published by Random House in 1977. Only *Freedomways* and the *New York Times* reviewed it; no other Black periodical, and not a single feminist periodical, acknowledged the book. It was an unexpected silence that pushed me to further re-examine my assumptions of community, since at the time I was a contributing editor for *First World* and *HooDoo* (both of them Black journals) and *Chrysalis* (a feminist magazine).

I decided to pretend that somebody wanted to know how I came to be a poet, and what I had in mind, poem by poem.

This essay was published by *Chrysalis*.

Nailed to my wooden bedroom door is a poem by Adrienne Rich, a response to my new book from the Black critic Stephen Henderson, a glossy of Monique Wittig and myself talking together, excitedly, a torn-out article on Alaska as an example of environmental crisis, a love poem from a friend, and a recent, angry limmerick that I wrote "after cleaning the house on a Sunday afternoon by myself, as usual." This particular door separates my room from the kitchen; it is seldom shut. On the floor around my bed you can find the poems of John Ashbery, a novel by Mishima, two books by Alta, the first issue of *Condi-*

tions, a recent issue of *Black Scholar*, and Jarrell's *Poetry and the Age.*

"What," I sometimes wonder, "am I trying to do, exactly?" I think that I am trying to keep myself free, that I am trying to become responsive and responsible to every aspect of my human being. I think that I am trying to learn whatever I can that will make freedom of choice an intelligent, increasing possibility. Often, these desires, these needs, translate into the sweltering sensation of a half-assed effort to explore and accomplish everything at once. But, thankfully, not always.

At first, say roughly from the age of seven through my mid-twenties, poetry was the inside dictator to whom I more or less simply submitted myself, writing down whatever the poem turned out to be, wording myself as precisely, and with whatever ambiguity, as was necessary in the interest of truthfulness. For example, the poem entitled "Pygmalion" came to me, entirely given, after reading Huxley's *Doors to Perception*, in my freshman year at Barnard. It begins:

blood mist bemuses meditation
bewilders stone cathedral sipping clemency to needs
derides impulsive incantations sacred golden full
removes ascendant pyres from raw hidden origins
despises skin simplicity which bled and bleeds in silence
young Christ   sweet Lord   avoided in austere enclosures

Exceptions to this quasi-automatic process were the regular exercises that I invented for myself so that I should feel competent, as regards craft, to write in the manner of Herrick, Shelley, Eliot, or whoever, and whenever. These disciplined emulations/transmutations absorbed a great part of my working time, as a poet, although I did not consider them achievements of any kind; they served as means, strictly, and not ends. I guess my theory was that if apprenticeship was essential to painting then apprenticeship was essential to being a poet, an identity I assumed from childhood with rather unquestioning, and even religious, feelings of sobriety. It is certain that I did not regard these studies as optional. All my life, the rule was that if you were Black you had to be twice as good/smart as anyone else just to get started. I was started, all right, but I felt it imperative to protect myself, my coming voice, from easy/categorical rejection.

Of course, preoccupation with one's self and with technique does not yield an art of interest to anyone else, necessarily, as I finally decided. In order to deserve the attention of people-out-there, I would have to concern myself with accessibility and with subjects of general consequence: indebtedness to parents, isolation, strangers, marriage, race, war, rage, love. I would have to decide, beforehand, the purpose of the poem. What did I want anybody else to see, smell, feel, understand? And, why? This last emerging concern centered me upon a conscious desire to change our environment, to scrape and ax away at the status quo. As this decision coincided approximately with the 1954 Supreme Court ruling, I found myself well supported; I was speeded forward, outside and beyond the simply personal, even as collective interests and collective action became the dominant public realities of the day. In addition, I was fortunate enough to be sponsored by the Academy of American Poets as a poet reading her works throughout the public school system of New York City—every level and every borough of the system. As you know, kids are pretty tough. And the repeated, regular, direct exposure to kids as an audience for my work irresistibly propelled me outward into new (for me) aesthetic values and new (for me) subjects just so I could hope to stand in front of them without being the biggest bore of the morning.

Although the musical potentiality of language persisted as a primary love and goal, from childhood, rhythm as vertical event, and/or rhythm as the cohesive structure of a poem only emerged as a central quest after I found myself face to face with children, and teenagers, who have a natural affinity for movement as in palpable momentum. For instance, the horizontal rhythms of Shelley, and the amazing music of "I bring fresh showers for the thirsting flowers,/From the seas and the streams;/I bear light shade for the leaves when laid/In their noonday dreams," in his poem "The Cloud," indelibly excited my ear to what I called the "Spanish" possibilities of English. And Shelley's

"Queen Mab," especially sections IV to VII, utterly persuaded me that you could write political poetry that would stand as legitimate as any other poetry, as in his lines: "All things are sold: the very light of Heaven/is venal; earth's unsparing gifts of love,/The smallest and most despicable things/That lurk in the abysses of the deep,/All objects of our life, even life itself..." But I had never seen rhythm and political concept merged into a vertical event. "In memoriam: Martin Luther King, Jr.," an excerpt of which follows, was perhaps my first attempt:

honey people murder mercy U.S.A.
the milkland turn to monsters teach
to kill to violate pull down destroy
the weakly freedom growing fruit
from being born

America

tomorrow yesterday rip rape
exacerbate despoil disfigure ...

And as far as changes in subject are concerned, while I did not make my "self" disappear, my self-conscious criterion became that of comprehensible relationship between the person (me) and the public, by which I meant either the reader and/or the public issue under treatment.

Toward the close of the sixties, I reconsidered, and decided that I wanted to aim for the achievement of a collective voice, that I wanted to speak as a community to a community, that to do otherwise was not easily defensible, nor useful, and would be, in any case, at variance with clarified political values I held as my own, by then. I think it was in 1973 that Radcliffe convened a Black Women's Conference, and invited me to be "the wrap-up" poet. With this function in mind, I conceived a poem about the collective experience of Black womanhood. Accordingly, some of the events within the poem would not necessarily reflect my personal history, but all of the events, and all of the personae, would represent my felt, collective perspective on our collective heritage and predicament. The poem that resulted,

"Gettin Down to Get Over: Dedicated to My Mother," was, in fact, a breakthrough for me, on several levels, simultaneously. I had the rare and extraordinary chance to test this collective voice upon some five hundred or so Black women sisters of mine. And, happily, they accepted the representation of their and my lives, in the poem that begins:

MOMMA MOMMA MOMMA

momma momma
mammy
nanny
granny
woman
mistress
sista

luv . . .

But a few years into the seventies, and I reconsidered again; aspirations toward a collective voice seemed to me conceitful, at least. Instead, I came to the idea of myself as ordinary. As I came to know other poets as friends, particularly other living Black poets—Clarence Major, Calvin Hernton, David Henderson—and other living women poets—Audre Lorde, Sonia Sanchez, Adrienne Rich, Susan Griffin—it did seem to me that we were all of us working on the same poem of a life of perpetual, difficult birth and that, therefore, I should trust myself in this way: that if I could truthfully attend to my own perpetual birth, if I could trace the provocations for my own voice and then trace its reverberations through love, Alaska, whatever, that then I could hope to count upon myself to be serving a positive and collective function, without pretending to be more than the one Black woman poet I am, as a matter of fact.

This last concept of my work remains the governing criterion, as I write these thoughts, tonight: to be accurate about myself, and to force my mind into a constantly expanding apprehension of my political and moral situation. Necessarily, this changed, ruling value has altered my attitudes about movement in poetry, and about comprehensibility. There is stillness, there is sometimes paralysis in my experience, and there is much that I do not understand and that I need to confront as the incoherency, the mystery, it may mean, or be, even ultimately. And as I wish to be truthful, so my poems must reflect these other elements of being, as well.

Besides conscious changes in the purpose perceived and, consequently, changes in the techniques explored in my work, there have been changes of influence and perspective at least equal in their determining importance. (Some sources of influence have remained unalterable, such as Shelley, and such as these lines by Coleridge: "Hence viper thoughts that coil about my mind/reality's dark dream/I turn from thee and listen to the wind/which long hath rav'd unnotic'd.") "Greatness" figured as a deeply motivating notion for me, throughout my childhood. I wanted to be "a great poet"; indeed, anything less than greatness, anything less than acknowledged excellence, did not interest me. And the poets pushed upon me by my father, before my tenth birthday, were the poets of the Scriptures, Shakespeare, Edgar Allan Poe, along with the dialect poetry of Paul Laurence Dunbar. And so I thought I recognized a rather serious dilemma: how could I become "a great poet," being female, and not much taken either with Dunbar's southern dialect or with Elizabethan English which were, both of them, altogether weird to my ears. I even pondered the fact that these four founts were dead, so to speak. That posed a clear difficulty that left me feeling uncomfortable, but not suicidal—except that their remoteness from my world and my language, coupled with their redoubtable acclaim, crippled my trust in my own sensibilities, coerced me into eclectic compulsions I had to struggle against, later, and generally delayed my creative embracing of my own, known life as the very stuff of my art.

In my twenties, the political—racist and sexist—factors involved in "literary acknowledgment" capsized my earlier respect for the concept of "greatness," and buried it; with the shattering of my political naiveté, I passed through a period of years during which I pretty much refused to read, or hear, any poetry that was not Black; I was no longer interested to become part of a tradition that dared to silence the poetry of my people. I could no longer countenance such standards as dared to reject the distinctively Black elements of our consciousness and our art. Margaret Walker, Robert Hayden, Langston Hughes were some of the Black poets whose work I most enjoyed. And there was the exquisite articulation of ambivalence that I very much admired in Le Roi Jones' "Dead Lecturer." And there was the astonishing, irrepressible beauty and force of the allegedly verbally deficient Black and Puerto Rican teenagers in Fort Greene, Brooklyn, with whom I had the privilege of working, for a few years, in our Saturday workshop that came to be known as The Voice of the Children. Consider this poem by thirteen-year-old Linda Curry which appeared in our book *The Voice of the Children.*

MY ENEMY

My Enemy is The World
The world hates me   it's trying
to get rid of me   Somebody
up there don't like me
Why I don't know
I've try to prove them
      wrong but it doesn't seem
to work
I don't know what to think
      or do I just
wonder till I find
what I am searching
for And then I will kill
the one who hates me.

More than anything else, it was the poetry of Linda Curry, it was the fighting for these kids, it was the living with them through inevitable insults in "white territory," it was the attempt to carry them through the unspeakably brutal year of 1968, that riveted my heart and mind to the preservation of Black English and to distinctively Black poetry. Indeed, my first novel, *His Own Where*, which was written entirely in Black English, was based upon two "regulars" of our workshop, and, of course, upon my own, personal life as a child growing up in Bedford-Stuyvesant.

Toward the end of my twenties, and continuing through my thirties, the poetry of women, contemporary and past, became fundamental to my spirit, and joined Black poetry as part of the literature I was willing to respect, and wanted to incorporate into my being. Emily Dickinson, Jane Cooper, Adrienne Rich, Audre Lorde, Marge Piercy, Alice Walker, Honor Moore are some of the women who have awakened me to another dimension of love, and of struggle.

At this point in time, I refuse nothing. I am concerned to keep myself open and aware of all that I can. Hence, while women's poetry (particularly today's poetry as it issues from the embattled lives of feminist poets and writers) occupies a first place of influence, and while Third World Poetry continues to function as the fundamental testimony I wish to serve, I do read and I do indeed listen to the poetry of white male poets: Ted Hughes, Charles Simic, David Ignatow, Charles Bukowski. (Neruda and Nicanor Parra are not "white," as far as I know.)

I think this present orientation, this perhaps catholicity of interest, if not always a matter of enthusiasm, reflects my changed perspective. I have moved from an infantile reception of the universe, as given, into a progressively political self-assertion that is now reaching beyond the limitations of a victim mentality. I choose to exist unafraid of my enemies; instead, I choose to become an enemy to my enemies. And I choose to believe that my enemies can either be vanquished or else converted into allies, into Brothers. And I choose to disregard the death-obsessed, extravagantly depressed and depressing doom-sayers around. As a woman, as a Black woman, as a Black woman poet and writer, I choose to believe that we, women and Third World peoples, will in fact succeed in saving ourselves, *and* our traditional assassins, from the meaning of their fear and their hatred. Even more deeply, I believe we can save ourselves from the power of our own fear and our own self-hatred.

This is my perspective, and this is my faith.

16 Old Stories: New Lives (1978)

Old Stories: New Lives was written as the keynote address for a Northwest Regional Conference convened by the Child Welfare League of America, in 1978.

When I thought about the children for whom I would be speaking, the much abused and embarrassing humility of my students at the S.U.N.Y. at Stony Brook, the desolate fixity of the Puerto Rican teenagers who sat on my stoop, on 20th Street in Manhattan, trying to make babies to the sound of plastic radios that they held against the broken glass savagery of the street, the torn-up gut quandaries of my son, a Black man at Harvard University, and the respectable brutality of a five-year-old's middle class parents rushed through me as one moan. I was burned by the hurt of the words racing through my mind and I wrote this piece from that familiar place: that feeling.

See Valerie. She is five. She is scared. She is white. She is very small. Her parents both graduated from Ivy League schools. She lives with them. See Valerie's house. It's a big place that cost a lot of money. Besides Valerie and her father and her mother, see the two dogs, see the aquarium, see the turtle, see the three or four hundred books, see the two bathrooms, see the garden, see the garage, see the big TV that Valerie looks at every day. See Valerie afraid. See Valerie alone. See Valerie by herself, thumb in her mouth, in front of the TV. Valerie does not play. Valerie does not giggle or laugh. Valerie is serious. She has to be. Nobody really likes Valerie. But what can she do about that? Where can she go? Everything that Valerie does is calculated for effect: at five she has become a desperate actress practicing various ways not to be herself, to be unreal—lying, smiling, screaming that she wants some cheese to eat when she is actually not hungry at all.

Valerie's mother does nothing much from one day to the next. She sits around the house, chain-smoking cigarettes, and reading the *New York Times*. The house is filthy and opulent. Valerie provides her with a current excuse from life as a nonparasitic adult: who will hire a middle-aged woman to do what, anyway? Valerie's mother is fond of saying, "In a minute," or "After I finish this cigarette," and then forgetting the promise she will therefore not keep, where Valerie is concerned. Or, Valerie's mother will suddenly yell at her daughter, "Keep your feet off the wall!" and then indulgently note that the dogs are on the dining room table, licking plates clean, as usual. See Valerie's feet; they are not on the wall.

Valerie's father is extremely overweight and what we used to categorize as "hen-pecked"; when he comes home after work, each night, he makes the dinner, does the dishes and, once in a while, lamely attempts to intercede, to make peace between his wife and his little girl. Mostly he affects a posture, an attitude of abstracted, hard-of-hearing indifference. He wishes he was dead. He will do anything to avoid the high-pitched explosions of his wife. It is his habit to call Valerie by pet names that are either scatological or that deliberately confuse his daughter with such animals as pigs.

See Valerie. She thinks that one day her mother may strangle her because her mother sometimes wants to strangle her, and says, "If you do that one more time I'll strangle you!" Valerie thinks that one day her father may let her drown in the bathtub or get hit by a car because he is so absent-minded and because, when her mother threatens to strangle her, her father says nothing, or else he walks out of the room.

See Valerie. Picture her, at five years old, trying to describe a Mack truck to people who have never seen one. How can she convey the size, the design, the weight of a Mack truck? Who will listen to her, anyone? She's five. She's very small. How can she express the terror, the horror of her life that is not her fault, her life that was somebody's mistake, somebody's doomed effort to prove that a dismal marriage could be redeemed by a baby: a new, an entirely new, but an entirely dependent life.

See Valerie: Where can she go?

When I was a child I never wanted to grow up. Now that I am grown, I look at the children and I think, "God help them to survive us, the big people in their lives." Mostly, of course, our children will not survive our habits of thinking, our failures of the spirit, our wreck of the universe into which we bring new life, as blithely as we do. Mostly, our children will resemble our own misery and spite and anger, because we give them no choice about it. In the name of motherhood and fatherhood and education and good manners, we threaten and suffocate and bind and ensnare and bribe and trick children into wholesale emulation of our ways. Indeed, originality is recognized as disobedience, pathology, incorrigible character and/or unlawful conduct to be prosecuted by the state. Departure from established modes of being is seldom perceived as innovative or valuably alternative or necessary or, in any wise, legitimate. At best, new behavior by the new people among us, the children, is perceived as something to patronize or to tolerate, knowing that the systematic force of our adult demands for slavelike mimicry will likely overcome rebellious inclination, soon enough. Soon enough for what? Soon enough to convert these new lives into old stories we should be mortified, by now, to hear.

When I was a child I never wanted to grow up because it was obvious that grownups were these very unhappy people. All the time they did things they didn't want to do. They went to work. They woke up early. They pretended to like neighbors. They stayed married. They had babies. They paid their income tax. They made sacrifices. They controlled themselves. And then there was my father, for example, who used to say, just before beating me, "This hurts me more than it will hurt you."

And I thought, "Why does he have to do this to himself, I mean, why does he have to do this to me?"

Certainly I did not want to remain a child, to remain powerless, that is. I wanted to grow so that I could take my revenge or so that I could decide things for myself, so that I could be different from my mother and my father. What I never realized was that, the longer I lived, the more similar I would become, the more I would lose my own ideas about being happy, about how to be happy. I would even lose the idea that it was good to be happy. And the only way I could change into somebody powerful was this: I had to imitate the powerful people around me. It was a circular dilemma that left me, thinking about it, grim to the point of blank staring at the ground or, as adults saw me, daydreaming, again.

Jackson is sixteen. He's Black. He lives in Detroit. So far this semester, he can stay out of school another week before the truant officer rings the bell and that mess about suspension becomes a crisis for his mother who doesn't know what to do with him. Jackson is not sure what he wants. At sixteen, the fact that he ever goes to school sets him outside the more than 60 percent national dropout rate for minority students, by the time they reach his age. In other words, most of his friends already hang on the streets, as a matter of course. There is no work. He can't figure it out. If there's no work, and if school is so ridiculous there's no point to wasting time inside that building, and if there's no work even for white college graduates, and if there's no work, and if he stays in the dumbassed vocational high school, or if he quits, there still won't be work and then how in the hell is he supposed to manage? What did anybody have in mind, bringing him into the world?

Across the street, there's Linda and her baby; she's feeding him french fries with ketchup on a piece of newspaper on the stoop. Linda is fourteen and don't know her ass from her elbow. Can't spell contraception right, but she's cute. And on the corner there's this old guy sitting next to a little kid could be his grandson or something and the old man holds this yellow Frisbee on his knees, perfectly still. They been like that, the boy and the old man, for more than an hour. Jackson figures don't nobody know the answers. What he needs is a couple bucks for a nickel bag and to hell with it. Or a car, maybe. Now how could he get his hands on a car?

Well we know how. We know the only probable way for Jackson to get a car. And we also probably have a vague idea about the perpetuating, the reinforcing general facts pertinent to his contemporaries, his family relatives. But do we know what it means about us that, ten years after the murder of Dr. King, the overall Black and minority unemployment rate has soared from 8 percent to more than 25 percent? Whom shall we hold accountable for the fact that, ten years after the bullet that killed the man who had a dream, more than 60 percent of all minority students will drop out of school with a fifth grade reading level? And what is the moral significance of the fact that, as of today, well over half of the minority peoples living in urban areas *perforce* endure dwellingspace legally identified as hazardous to life and limb?

As a child growing up in Bedford-Stuyvesant I could hardly understand why it was that the garbage was not collected, the mail not delivered, ambulance service not available, and police protection impossible, but I did surmise, like Valerie, that nobody really liked me or any of the people in my community. I did surmise that somebody must hate all of us because in order to buy food that was not stale and ugly and overpriced, and in order to attend a school that was not horrible and crippling and dangerous, my people, and we were all of us Black, had to travel far into white communities where we were not welcome, in order to secure acceptable string beans, acceptable math instruction.

And while it would not have helped me, it would not have rescued me, to know that one reason my father beat me to the extent of occasional scar tissue was because he himself felt beaten and he himself felt bullied and despised by strangers more powerful than he would ever be—strangers he felt he could not defy, directly, except at the cost of his pitiful livelihood. While it would not have saved me from the nightmare experience of his brutality, is it not apparent to me today, is it not crystalline to all of us, that the pain and the grief, the racist and sexist destruction of our possibilities, the incessant competition, the humiliating uncertainty, impotence, and disappointment of our grownup existence cannot but punish those who are yet weaker than we: our children? Is it not evident that they are least able to defend themselves who most depend upon us? And when we turn upon these small ones, whether they be white or Black or male or female or cursed by imposed poverty or smothered by middle-class vacuities, when we cannot control our bitterness and we strike out against the only safe targets for our own anguish and our mumbling wrath, when we whip or castigate our children just short of the absurdly ultimate, gross definition of child abuse, where can they go? Each and every day, for example, in New York City, police estimate that there are 20,000 "runaways": *twenty thousand!* Nor do these young people enjoy any protection of their rights as human beings, under present law. Nobody runs away from safety, from a truly supportive, respectful, open situation. And, nevertheless, the law assumes that these children are wrong to have run away; indeed, runaways are adjudged to be criminals. The law does not allow that the homes of these youngsters may be what's wrong. And we, the grownups in charge, we do not see fit to create an alternative, humanely defensible shelter for children who take the drastic, terrifying step of running away— with no rights before the law, no means, and no lawful opportunities to become decently self-sufficient.

In his brilliant work, *Pathways to Madness*, Jules Henry demonstrated in so-called case after case, that it is not the child who is crazy, the child who is wrong. Repeatedly it is the adult-constructed circumstance into which he or she is bound, that guarantees the shift from childlike efforts to cope with psychotic patterns of behavior to children suffering psychosis, as we term the end result—little people who have collapsed in confrontation with the evils of adult disease.

When you consider that more than 40 percent of all marriages end in divorce, that more than 60 percent of all divorced fathers default on child support payments, when you spend an afternoon observing the snarling interaction between mothers and children in your nearest, suburban shopping mall, it must be unarguably clear to you that our runaways may well be the backbone courageous among our kids: the ones who will risk hunger and forced prostitution and jail and death, in order to say NO to this overwhelming suffocation and victimizing, adult defeat into which they have been trapped, by dint of being born.

We look at the pretty girl hitchhiking on the highway and we shake our heads. When we heard about the hippies, the barely more than boys and girls who decided to try something different—to live in tents and to plant tomatoes and to bake bread and to share everything and to revel in the sunlight and in sex and to hardly ever change their clothes—we laughed at them. Smug in our certain awareness that the pretty girl would be/should be raped by asking for a ride, smug that communal life must be more difficult even than nuclear family life, which we know, to our very nerve endings, is disastrous, we condemned them, our children, for seeking a different future. We hated them for their flowers, for their love, and for their unmistakable rejection of every hideous, mistaken compromise that we had made throughout our hollow, money-bitten, frightened, adult lives.

And when the ridicule did not deter them, and when our condemnation did not succeed, and when these children whom we wanted to belittle and to warp into our own image, when they turned to look at us with wide stare, and when they, our children, soberly cried out against the atrocity of our power— the racism and the sexism and the imperialism of our extremely grownup preoccupation—when our children cried out against the murder that we perpetuated throughout the world, when they shouted out Stop The War, when they screamed aloud because our lying became unbearable to them, when they screamed against our invasion of Cambodia, we killed them. At Kent State, eight years ago, we killed our own children. We finally went ahead and made plain the substance of our hanging threat to all the lives of all of our children. If you do not do as we have done, if you do not continue what we do, we who have brought you here, we will take you out; we who feed and clothe you and teach you the words that you use, the name that is your name, we will destroy you even unto death.

And the grownup gentry rose to the occasion of Kent State. By the hundreds, letters came to the bereaved parents of the murdered children saying, "If she was my daughter, I would have killed her myself."

I remember the morning after the Cambodia invasion. I was on campus, at Sarah Lawrence College. My students came to me, hysterical, tears running every which way down their cheeks and into their own mouths. "Well, we have to do something to stop this," I said. "No," they answered me. "No. They won't listen to us. Who are we?" they asked, "Who are we?" And when we received the news about the murder of four students at Kent State, believe me the shivering, terrified, paralyzed silence among my students was absolute. And I, a grownup among them, what could I say to them now?

Later that afternoon, I walked quietly around the campus remembering two years earlier, when Dr. King was assassinated, and the Black and Puerto Rican teenagers of our creative writing group in Brooklyn sat together, stunned, that weekend. Finally, Wayne, a large boy with a fancy for gold chains, said, stammering, "Well, what do you think? Will they kill all of us?"

I do not know. Will we kill all of us? Can any one of us here, tonight, answer that question with any reasonable grounds for assurance? Given the damaged air and the spoiling waters and the ravaged land of our environment, given the relentless commitment to power and to weaponry, given the unmitigated reverence for capital good and private property versus human life itself, given the billionfold hungering of our brothers and sisters on earth, the actual starvation and famine following from deliberate, adult policies of political and economic concerns, alone, given Valerie and Jackson, I do not know. Will we kill all of us?

At the S.U.N.Y. at Stony Brook, where I have been teaching this past year, students have told me, at last, that when the semester began, when I sat in a circle among them, when I said, this is not my class, this is our class, I do not want to hear what I think, I need to know what you think, the students told me, finally, that they were dumfounded. They thought it must be a set-up or else a jive undertaking. What did I mean, a powerful adult among them, when I insisted that I wanted to learn with them, to hear what they had to say? As a teacher it is invariably the fact that my primary challenge is, year after year, to convince our children that they know something we need to know, and that their own feelings are important, at least as important as those adult values they must struggle against and, somehow, survive, if they will ever be certified as legitimate human beings. And so it is not surprising to me that only this year, after so long, do we find campus demonstrations across the country, once again—student rebellions against the monstrosity of South Africa and everything South Africa represents.

Can you persuade Valerie or Jackson that anything in South Africa is more horrendous than her or his particular and apparently inescapable doom? Who would dare to try to convince these children that their own jeopardy is one whit less than the spectacular derogation of life implicit and explicit in the South African holocaust?

I ask you: Who among us is competent to raise our children? Who among us is competent to have a love affair? Who among us is competent, who among us is strong enough and sure enough and safe enough and happy enough to truly love and protect those who are smaller and weaker than we are? Who among us is competent enough in genuine life science and life art so that we can foster and appreciate and calmly explore the potentiality of a different way of doing things, a different way of seeing things, a different, a new way of being at home in the world?

I am convinced that our children pose the question whereby we must justify our power over their lives, or give it up. It seems tragically evident that we have to give it up: our power, our coercion of new life into old stories; we have to solicit and cultivate and respect major differences of behavior and habit and perspective as they emerge from our new life, our children.

We have to invent alternatives to our own homes and the villainous, defiling streets beyond, for our backbone courageous kids who want out. These alternatives have to support the profoundly serious implication of our being rejected by our young people.

And why not? Can we not learn from our children because we cannot believe that we are capable of having created a new life that may save our own? Are we bankrupt of self-love to the degree that we cannot have faith in the innocence and the willingness and the tenderly discovering and perpetual energy and excitement of our young people? We have brought them into life and, verily, we can take that life away. We have suffered through this, our only life, and here it can come to a halt: we do not need to suffer the children to come and to die as we have come, as we are dying. But for that, we will have to rescue Valerie and Jackson from ourselves, from the tragedy of our own making.

To rescue our children we will have to let them save us from the power we embody: we will have to trust the very difference that they forever personify. And we will have to allow them the choice, without fear of death: that they may come and do likewise or that they may come and that we will follow them, that a little child will lead us back to the child we will always be, vulnerable and wanting and hurting for love and for beauty.

See Valerie. See you and see me:
Where can she go?

17 Where Is the Love? (1978)

The 1978 National Black Writers Conference at Howard University culminated with an extremely intense public seminar entitled *Feminism and the Black Woman Writer*. This was an historic, unprecedented event tantamount to conceding that, under such a heading, there might be something to discuss! Acklyn Lynch, Sonia Sanchez, Barbara Smith, and myself were the panelists chosen to present papers to the standing room only audience. I had been asked, also, to moderate the proceedings and therefore gave the opening statement, *Where Is the Love?*, which was later published in *Essence* magazine.

From phone calls and other kinds of gossip, I knew that the very scheduling of this seminar had managed to divide people into camps prepared for war. Folks were so jumpy, in fact, that when I walked into the theater I ran into several Black feminists and then several Black men who, I suppose, just to be safe, had decided not to speak to anyone outside the immediate circle of supportive friends they had brought with them.

The session was going to be hot. Evidently, feminism was being translated into lesbianism, into something interchangeable with lesbianism, and the taboo on feminism, within the Black intellectual community, had long been exceeded in its orthodox severity only by the taboo on the subject of the lesbian. I say within the intellectual Black community, because, minus such terms as *feminist* and *lesbian*, the phenomena of self-directed Black women or the phenomena of Black women loving other women have hardly been uncommon, let alone unbelievable, events to Black people not privy to theoretical strife about correct and incorrect Black experience.

This blurring of issues seemed to me incendiary and obnoxious. Once again, the Black woman writer would be lost to view as issues of her sex life claimed public attention at the expense of intellectual and aesthetic focus upon her work. Compared to the intellectual and literary criticism accorded to James Baldwin and Richard Wright, for example, there is damned little attention paid to their bedroom activities. In any case, I do not believe that feminism is a matter, first or last, of sexuality.

The seminar was going to be a fight. It was not easy to prepare for this one. From my childhood in Brooklyn I knew that your peers would respect you if you could hurt somebody. Much less obvious was how to elicit respect as somebody who felt and who meant love.

I wanted to see if it was possible to say things that people believe they don't want to hear, without having to kick ass and without looking the fool for holding out your hand. Was there some way to say, to insist on, each, perhaps disagreeable, individual orientation and nonetheless leave the union of Black men and Black women, as a people, intact? I felt that there had to be: If the individual cannot exist then who will be the people?

I expected that we, Black panelists and audience, together, would work out a way to deal, even if we didn't want to deal. And that's what happened, at Howard. We did. Nobody walked out. Nobody stopped talking. The session ended because we ran out of time.

———————

As I think about anyone or any thing—whether history or literature or my father or political organizations or a poem or a film—as I seek to evaluate the potentiality, the life-supportive commitment/possibilities of anyone or any thing, the decisive question is, always, *where is the love?* The energies that flow from hatred, from negative and hateful habits and attitudes and dogma do not promise something good, something I would choose to cherish, to honor with my own life. It is always the love, whether we look to the spirit of Fannie Lou Hamer, or to the spirit of Agostinho Neto, it is always the love that will carry action into positive new places, that will carry your own nights and days beyond demoralization and away from suicide.

I am a feminist, and what that means to me is much the same as the meaning of the fact that I am Black: it means that I must undertake to love myself and to respect myself as though my very life depends upon self-love and self-respect. It means that I must everlastingly seek to cleanse myself of the hatred and the contempt that surrounds and permeates my identity, as a woman, and as a Black human being, in this particular world of ours. It means that the achievement of self-love and self-respect will require inordinate, hourly vigilance, and that I am entering my soul into a struggle that will most certainly transform the experience of all the peoples of the earth, as no other movement can, in fact, hope to claim: because the movement into self-love, self-respect, and self-determination is the movement now galvanizing the true, the unarguable majority of human beings everywhere. This movement explicitly demands the testing of the viability of a moral idea: that the health, the legitimacy of any status quo, any governing force, must be measured according to the experiences of those who are, comparatively, powerless. Virtue is not to be discovered in the conduct of the strong vis-à-vis the powerful, but rather it is to be found in our behavior and policies affecting those who are different, those who are weaker, or smaller than we. How do the strong, the powerful, treat children? How do we treat the aged among us? How do the strong and the powerful treat so-called minority members of the body politic? How do the powerful regard women? How do they treat us?

Easily you can see that, according to this criterion, the overwhelming reality of power and government and tradition is evil, is diseased, is illegitimate, and deserves nothing from us—no loyalty, no accommodation, no patience, no understanding—except a clear-minded resolve to utterly change this total situation and, thereby, to change our own destiny.

142

As a Black woman, as a Black feminist, I exist, simultaneously, as part of the powerless and as part of the majority
peoples of the world in two ways: I am powerless as compared
to any man because women, per se, are kept powerless by men/
by the powerful; I am powerless as compared to anyone white
because Black and Third World peoples are kept powerless by
whites/by the powerful. I am the majority because women constitute the majority gender. I am the majority because Black
and Third World peoples constitute the majority of life on this
planet.

And it is here, in this extreme, inviolable coincidence of my
status as a Black feminist, my status as someone twice stigma-
tized, my status as a Black woman who is twice kin to the
despised majority of all the human life that there is, it is here,
in that extremity, that I stand in a struggle against suicide. And
it is here, in this extremity, that I ask, of myself, and of any
one who would call me *sister, Where is the love?*

The love devolving from my quest for self-love and self-
respect and self-determination must be, as I see it, something
you can verify in the ways that I present myself to others, and
in the ways that I approach people different from myself. How
do I reach out to the people I would like to call my sisters and
my brothers and my children and my lovers and my friends?
If I am a Black feminist serious in the undertaking of self-love,
then it seems to me that the legitimate, the morally defensible
character of that self-love should be such that I gain and gain
and gain in the socio-psychic strength needed so that I may,
without fear, be able and willing to love and respect women,
for example, who are not like me: women who are not feminists, women who are not professionals, women who are not
as old or as young as I am, women who have neither job nor
income, women who are not Black.

And it seems to me that the socio-psychic strength that should
follow from a morally defensible Black feminism will mean that
I become able and willing, without fear, to love and respect all
men who are willing and able, without fear, to love and respect
me. In short, if the acquirement of my self-determination is
part of a worldwide, an inevitable, and a righteous movement,

then I should become willing and able to embrace more and more of the whole world, without fear, and also without self-sacrifice.

This means that, as a Black feminist, I cannot be expected to respect what somebody else calls self-love if that concept of self-love requires my suicide to any degree. And this will hold true whether that somebody else is male, female, Black, or white. My Black feminism means that you cannot expect me to respect what somebody else identifies as the Good of The People, if that so-called Good (often translated into *manhood* or *family* or *nationalism*) requires the deferral or the diminution of my self-fulfillment. We *are* the people. And, as Black women, we are most of the people, any people, you care to talk about. And, therefore, nothing that is Good for The People is good unless it is good for me, as I determine myself.

When I speak of Black feminism, then, I am speaking from an exacerbated consciousness of the truth that we, Black women, huddle together, miserably, on the very lowest levels of the economic pyramid. We, Black women, subsist among the most tenuous and least likely economic conditions for survival.

When I speak of Black feminism, then, I am not speaking of sexuality. I am not speaking of heterosexuality or lesbianism or homosexuality or bisexuality; whatever sexuality anyone elects for his or her pursuit is not my business, nor the business of the state. And, furthermore, I cannot be persuaded that one kind of sexuality, as against another, will necessarily provide for the greater happiness of the two people involved. I am not talking about sexuality. I am talking about love, about a steady-state deep caring and respect for every other human being, a love that can only derive from a secure and positive self-love.

As a Black woman/feminist, I must look about me, with trembling, and with shocked anger, at the endless waste, the endless suffocation of my sisters: the bitter sufferings of hundreds of thousands of women who are the sole parents, the mothers of hundreds of thousands of children, the desolation and the futility of women trapped by demeaning, lowest-paying occupations, the unemployed, the bullied, the beaten, the bat-

144

tered, the ridiculed, the slandered, the trivialized, the raped, and the sterilized, the lost millions and multimillions of beautiful, creative, and momentous lives turned to ashes on the pyre of gender identity. I must look about me and, as a Black feminist, I must ask myself: *Where is the love?* How is my own lifework serving to end these tyrannies, these corrosions of sacred possibility?

As a Black feminist poet and writer I must look behind me with trembling, and with shocked anger, at the fate of Black women writers until now. From the terrible graves of a traditional conspiracy against my sisters in art, I must exhume the works of women writers and poets such as Georgia Douglas Johnson (who?).

In the early flush of the Harlem Renaissance, Georgia Johnson accomplished an astonishing, illustrious life experience. Married to Henry Lincoln Johnson, U.S. Recorder of Deeds in Washington, D.C., the poet, in her own right, became no less than Commissioner of Conciliation for the U.S. Department of Labor *(who was that again? Who?)*. And she, this poet, furthermore enjoyed the intense, promotional attention of Dean Kelley Miller, here at Howard, and W. E. B. DuBois, and William Stanley Braithwaite, and Alain Locke. And she published three volumes of her own poetry and I found her work in Countee Cullen's anthology, *Caroling Dusk*, where, Countee Cullen reports, she, Georgia Douglas Johnson, thrived as a kind of Gwendolyn Brooks, holding regular Saturday night get-togethers with the young Black writers of the day.

And what did this poet of such acclaim, achievement, connection, and generosity, what did this poet have to say in her poetry, and who among us has ever heard of Georgia Douglas Johnson? And is there anybody in this room who can tell me the name of two or three other women poets from the Harlem Renaissance? And why did she die, and why does the work of all women die with no river carrying forward the record of such grace? How is it the case that whether we have written novels or poetry or whether we have raised our children or cleaned and cooked and washed and ironed, it is all dismissed as "women's work"; it is all, finally, despised as nothing important, and there is no trace, no echo of our days upon the earth?

Why is it not surprising that a Black woman as remarkably capable and gifted and proven as Georgia Douglas Johnson should be the poet of these pathetic, beggarly lines:

I'm folding up my little dreams
within my heart tonight
And praying I may soon forget
the torture of their sight
        "My Little Dreams"

How long, how long will we let the dreams of women serve merely to torture and not to ignite, to enflame, and to ennoble the promise of the years of every lifetime? And here is Georgia Douglas Johnson's poem "The Heart of a Woman":

The heart of a woman goes forth with the dawn,
As a lovebird, softwinging, so restlessly on,
Afar o'er life's turrets and vales does it roam
In the wake of those echoes the heart calls home.

The heart of a woman falls back with the night
And enters some alien cage in its plight,
And tries to forget it has dreamed of the stars,
While it breaks, breaks, breaks on the sheltering bars.

And it is against such sorrow, and it is against such suicide, and it is against such deliberated strangulation of the possible lives of women, of my sisters, and of powerless peoples—men and children—everywhere, that I work and live, now, as a feminist trusting that I will learn to love myself well enough to love you (whoever you are), well enough so that you will love me well enough so that we will know exactly where is the love: that it is here, between us, and growing stronger and growing stronger.

18 Against the Wall (1978)

"Against the Wall" was published in *Seven Days*, 1978.

Above the sidestreets of Pretoria, the grainfields of Angola, the cracked earth of Soweto, there is, tonight, a full moon hanging heavily, and vague. And bright above the Blarney Rose Bar, Elba's Beauty Parlor, Butler Lumber, the Chemical Bank, and the Salvation Army building on Manhattan's 14th Street, there is the same full moon that, somewhere else, is pulling at the ocean for a washaway spectacular, corrosive at the edges of all territory.

Nothing unusual: The writer leaves the house and heads into the evening, outside, for a walk to clear the mind. And what about that? Is there anything peculiar in that act? Well, yes: The writer is a woman, and Black, besides. Consequently the act of taking a walk means that she, this writer, will be perceived as a provocative/irresponsible/loose/insubordinate creature on the streets, by herself, moving along as though she had a natural right to wander around, after dark.

Why does she do this thing, this apparently forbidden, extremely hazardous thing of walking on the streets, by herself? Maybe it's an emergency; she needs a prescription filled for her two-year-old son. Or maybe it's a mission of mercy for a suicidal friend. No? She just wants to mail letters at the post office, or think about God, or exercise her body, or sort her ideas and

147

feelings about what's happening in Southern Africa or just look at that moon!

If she's raped, if guys on the corners molest her innate sovereignty by making obscene remarks and noises as she passes by, if a bunch of punks decide to mug and mutilate her person, people will say: But why was she there? And I will answer: Why in the world should she be anywhere else?

I am here, wherever you find me, from Baltimore to Johannesburg, because I do really exist and because I have this notion that I have as much right to be wherever I am, whenever I choose to be, as you do. Indeed, throughout most of the earth, I/First World Peoples/women (who, after all, remain the *sine qua non* of human existence, as well as the majority gender), have more right, more legitimate claim to space and to unmolested liberty in space, than any other segment of the species.

And, tonight, the distinctions escape me. What is the difference between demanding that I carry "a pass," a certificate of permission to stand on my feet, and terrorist curfews imposed upon my movements because I am female?

But we, women and Black and First World Peoples, have become accustomed to the concept of rape: our bodies, our coloring, the structure of our genes, the violated boundaries of our lands, the forced extinction of our leaders and our dreams, the derogation of our singular beauty, our singular art, the systematic suffocation of our children, the social sterilization of our minds and the literal sterilization of our womb; these testify to our familiarity with rape.

Of course, rape is not new. In a way, that is the meaning of my identity: I have been raped. Somebody stronger than I am will attempt, yet again, and again, to maim and to desecrate my inalienable right to self-determination. He will claim that I was "asking for it" because I was attractive and alone and strange enough to behave as though I should be free to be myself. Or he will claim that he was invited to destroy the villages of my people, and that he was invited by the "legitimate" members of my family. Or he will claim that he had to invade and conquer my home because I was friendly with Cubans or other kinds of problematic types who were misleading my infantile

148

mentality. He will say he couldn't control himself. Or he will say I wanted him to do it. Or he will say he was saving me from myself, or for democracy, or something. He will certainly not be speechless: Patriarchal/western civilization is big on words. How else can you lie?

And the moon is full, everywhere, tonight: Southern Africa will become a haven, a situation of supreme safety for the multitudes now suffering rape. And here, in Manhattan, the streets will become a refuge, an agreeable alternative to the house for this particular Black woman, and for women generally, and do you know why I say that with so much calm?

Because all of us who are comparatively powerless, because we have decided that if you interfere, if you seek to intrude, if you undertake to terrorize and to subjugate and to stifle even one moment more of these, our only lives, we will take yours, or die, trying.

It's 12:30 A.M. and now I am going out, by myself, to put this in the mailbox, three blocks away. And, listen: I am not afraid.

19 In the Valley of the Shadow of Death (1978)

After an enormous, dirty fight, in fact, after the most disillusioning fight I have ever waged with editors, the "left" magazine *Seven Days* reluctantly published this story, this other side of the story of Black and white conflict in Brooklyn.

I was therefore appalled when I finally saw the cover of the issue that carried my report. On the cover, the story was advertised as "Blacks Against Hassidic Jews!" Since the immutable fact of that conflict was that upward of thirty Hassidic Jews attacked a Black boy, beating him into a critical state of coma, this editorial liberty violated every canon of ethical journalism. On the same ethical level, the editors of *Seven Days* printed this lie: "We asked Black poet June Jordan to report on the situation in her childhood neighborhood."

It seems to me that my whole life has been regularized by the apparently normal events of white/police violence against the Black community. Over and over and over again a child is killed by police because he is a Black boy. Sometimes it gets to the point that, when my son is around the house and I leave on an errand by myself, when I come back the first thing I do is to call, "Christopher?" I have to know: Is he all right?

One year after the police murder of Arthur Miller and the Hassidic assault upon Victor Rhodes, I got the chance, through a fellowship to Yaddo, to write a full-length drama, *The*

Issue, about freedom, police violence, and Black life. Early on, the hero of this play, Lloyd Wilson, makes this statement:

> They want to keep score! (Furious and slow and clear).
> Look at this garbage. All the way back to 1964. Then it
> was that pig, in Manhattan, Lieutenant Gilligan. Shot the
> kid who was fooling around with a *water* gun. And then
> there was Newark: Did you ever see that cover of *Life*
> magazine: Black boy bleeding to death on the street.
> Cops shot him through the back of the head. The kid
> was running with a six-pack. Of beer. Every mothafuck-
> ing year they do this, three/four times, at a minimum.
> All you got to do is let it be Christmas or Thanksgiving
> or spring or summer or Monday or Sunday and they act
> like killers on the loose, complete with license. But we!
> We getting good at funerals/funeral oratory. Good at
> rallies. Good at speeches and quotes for the press. It's
> a ritual: They murder our children. And what do we do
> about it? We cry real hard real loud. Then it's over:
> That's that. If I was a pig, behind all of that crying for
> all of that dying, I would blow away a nigga a day. Why
> the hell not.

I wrote this play in June and July, 1979. In August, Brooklyn police murdered Luis Baez, shooting him sixteen times. My friends, Alexis DeVeaux and Gwendolen Hardwick, and I went to a Brooklyn rally held to protest the killings. After the rally, approximately one thousand demonstrators followed Reverend Herbert Daughtry on a peaceful march through the streets, chanting *a people united can never be defeated*. The police rioted, driving police cars into the crowds and chasing unarmed demonstrators with drawn guns. We literally crawled across the concrete sidewalks to safety.

One year later, 1980, the courts ruled that no indictment of the Hassidic suspects was possible due to "insufficient identi-fication." No police were indicted in the murder of Arthur Miller.

Two months later, Miami police beat Arthur MacDuffie to

death, for a traffic violation. The media seemed surprised by the violence of the response of the Black community in Miami. Do not be surprised.

I say he will live.
This child of my people, this boy of sixteen, barely alive: his brain and his body comatose in agony since he fell prey to organized white violence: This Victor Rhodes, son of the streets and the underground dreams and the upfront terror of Black-folk everywhere:
I say he will live.

> "Yea, though I walk through the valley
> of the shadow of death . . ."

Ten years after the assassination of The Civil Rights Era we, Black people, find ourselves outside the door to the hospital ward where one Black life, the very remnant breath of Victor Rhodes, hovers in the shadow of death. More than three weeks ago, this Black child suffered a massive assault, a beating so savage, so apparently "professional," as his mother terms it (shuddering as she utters the word) that, even should he regain consciousness and one day be released from supremely constant and intensive care, it is not certain whether his survival will signify more than the victory of a living death.

The ultimate uncertainty of Victor's life is the same as the question basic to all Black people, today: If we do survive, then what will be the quality, the potential of our perseverence? Given the precipitous decline in the well-being of Black people during the last decade, given a triple increase in overall minority unemployment, a 50 percent increase in the high school dropout rate of minority students, coast to coast (e.g., from 40 percent in 1968 to 60 percent in 1978), given the California landslide of Proposition 13, the equivocal but plainly retreating resolve of the Supreme Court vis-à-vis Bakke and the University of

California at Davis, a national forecast for Black America would certainly be harrowing, if realistic.

In Victor's section of this country, the nerve endings of every Black man, woman, and child have been singed to tinderstuff. There are the inevitable results of such national statistics that, more than anyone else, Black people must withstand: higher crime rates, grossly deteriorated city services, and the consequent destruction of community morale. But, in addition, Black areas of Brooklyn have witnessed a tide of terrorist white violence such that South Africa and Mississippi arise, repeatedly, in casual discussions of the state of things.

Only go back as far as Thanksgiving, 1977, when Police Officer Torsney shot fifteen-year-old Randolph Evans in the head, and killed him. Randy, seeing officers leave his apartment building, had asked the cop a question, "Did you go into Apartment 7-D?" The bullet was Torsney's reply. That murder occurred in the East New York section of Brooklyn. Torsney was later acquitted by an all white jury on a plea of "insanity." His defense argued that he was subject to mental defects consequent to epileptic seizure. Officials of The Greater New York Chapter of the Epilepsy Foundation unanimously denounced the defense for virulent misleading of the public, but the verdict was already a matter of deed.

Activist Black leaders, principally the Rev. Herbert Daughtry, of The House of the Lord's Pentecostal Church, attempted to channel Black horror and sorrow into political protests such as an economic boycott of downtown Brooklyn stores, at Christmas time. On June 14, still struggling against the indifference of City Hall, Daughtry was stunned by the call he received, telling him of the murder of Arthur Miller, a highly respected, Black civic leader of Bedford-Stuyvesant, who was "subdued" by some sixteen policemen during an argument about the validity of a driver's license. Miller and his brother, Samuel, stood on one side of this dispute, and sixteen police plus a "Model Cities' cadet" stood on the other. As the debate developed, according to numerous eyewitnesses, Miller was handcuffed and made to kneel on the sidewalk, while the policemen whacked and kicked and, evidently, strangled him. According to the official police

153

report, "On the way to the 77th precinct, the officers noticed that Arthur Miller appeared to be unconscious." They then drove him to St. Mary's Hospital (although Brooklyn Jewish Hospital was just a block away) and there he was pronounced Dead on Arrival.

Huge headlines in the next day's papers could scarcely reflect the intensity of the dread and the anger that bolted throughout Black areas of Brooklyn; that evening, a rally was held and the theme of unity raised as a primary need for the sake of self-defense. By morning, Rev. Daughtry and all the rest of New York City awoke to the news that, as the New York *Post* reported it: "50 VIGILANTES STOMP A BLACK, 16." By "vigilantes," reference was being made to the Hassidic Jewish patrol of Crown Heights (a community that is 75 percent Black and less than 25 percent white) maintained by federal LEAA funds amounting to $160,000, yearly. The youth referred to was Victor Rhodes, *is* Victor Rhodes. Two Hassidic men were placed in bail of $70,000 each, charged with attempted murder. The complaint of Police Officer Michael Costello, 71st Precinct, states, "On June 16, 1978, at 12:25 A.M., in front of 1307 Union Street, Crown Heights, that the defendants, in concert with 30 to 50 *(fifty)* others, not apprehended, attempted to murder Mr. Rhodes, by kicking and stomping him."

When I interviewed Rabbi Yisroel Rosenfeld, a much quoted spokesman for the Lubavitcher Hassidim (the Hassidic sect prevailing in Crown Heights), Rosenfeld complained that these "incidents" were not "related"; to him, what happens in Bedford-Stuyvesant is properly seen as irrelevant to what happens in Crown Heights. (His reasoning reminded me of the colonialist jigsaw of Africa, which completely ignores, which deliberately seeks to subvert, those factors of Black experience that provide for a unified perspective and cultural history.) Indeed, I did not know, at the time of my interview with Rabbi Rosenfeld, the rather seamy facts of gerrymandering that resulted in the redefinition of Crown Heights, two years ago, so that the Lubavitcher Hassidim should achieve an effective political hegemony within their new confines.

Black physician Dr. Vernon Cave, a resident of Crown Heights

—no matter how you define its geography—for more than forty years, and also Chairman of the Board of Directors of Bedford-Stuyvesant Restoration Corporation, describes that redistricting as the time when "the Board of Estimate broke the law." Explaining that two of the three guidelines governing decisions to redistrict were clearly violated, Dr. Cave remains bitterly indignant as regards a political process vulnerable to such untoward manipulation: There was money involved—a lot of federal funds; and there was power involved—a mysterious degree of Hassidic leverage upon every level of government, leverage unimaginable even to so distinguished and influential a man as Dr. Cave.

But, while Rabbi Rosenfeld busied himself with territorial niceties, and while he gave me an account of the "Vic Rhodes incident" that quite contradicts an earlier account he had released to the press some days before (with equal embellishment and stentorian style), Black people, everywhere the news became available, assumed the hushed behavior of the hunted down: it would seem to be open season on Blackfolk. Perhaps our comparative silence since "the sixties" encouraged our enemies to believe that there was, in fact, no limit to the degradation and the depredations we would endure, without resistance? When I say "everywhere," I do not exaggerate. The following is an excerpt from a taped interview with Mr. Oauattara, Executive Secretary of the O.A.U., at the United Nations, June 27, 1978:

Have we heard any comment from the White House, from President Carter, regarding the death of Arthur Miller, and the (attempted) beating to death of Victor Rhodes? . . . If you will remember . . . when the death of Stephen Biko took place: Well, as I read what happened to Arthur Miller . . . the parallel is so significant. It is like a tragic coincidence.

"In the presence of mine enemies . . ."

The night of the Hassidic attack upon Victor Rhodes, he was walking his girlfriend home from a party to which he planned

155

to return. His friend lived opposite the main Hassidic synagogue on Eastern Parkway. He had to return to the party because his godsister was there, waiting for his escort back to the home and legal guardian they shared, some few blocks away. It is inconceivable that Vic struck "one of the boys" (i.e., Yeshiva students, in version one, according to Rabbi Rosenfeld) or that he or that "somebody" struck "an elderly Jew" (version two, according to the same authority) because no one living in Crown Heights makes any mistake about the paramilitary Hassidic control of Eastern Parkway in the vicinity of number 770, the address of the World Headquarters of the Lubavitch Hassidim. According to Captain Katz of the 71st Precinct, this Hassidic sect numbers a million and a half followers throughout the world, and its nucleus, opposite the home of Victor Rhodes' companion, has been characterized, since 1966, by a seven-day-a-week, 24-hour-a-day NYPD patrol car, manned by two police officers. The same remarkable protection has been the privilege of the head Lubavitch rabbi's private home, two blocks south. (Responding to the outcry against the egregious treatment enjoyed by the Hassidim, Mayor Koch last week ordered the vigil ended, only to be apparently defied by his Police Commissioner, who said this status quo would be maintained until "an alternative plan of protection with routine patrols" could be devised. It is interesting to note that the taxpayer cost of such singular services, since 1966, amounts to more than four million dollars; when last have you heard of comparable moneys made available for jobs for Black kids Victor's age, for instance?)

It is unlikely that Victor Rhodes would have chosen to cross the Parkway and thereby pass through patently Hassidic turf. The Black gynecologist Dr. Rufus A. Nichols and his wife, Janet, who live with their family just eight or nine doors down from "770," readily recount varieties of harassment they suffer as neighbors to the Hassidim. Since police, at the request of the Hassidim, unannounced, and regularly, barricade the public service road of Eastern Parkway, which is the means whereby Dr. and Mrs. Nichols must reach their home/office/driveway, and since Mrs. Nichols herself was arrested, and spent the night in jail, eight years ago, because, on her way home from marketing with the car, she found access to her home blocked by police barricades and, in exasperation, left her car to remove said impediments, in order to reach her home and her four children awaiting her return, and since her husband was performing emergency surgery at Brooklyn Jewish Hospital and, thus, there was no way to advise him of the absurdist nightmare in progress, the Nicholses have nothing really pleasant to say about the ongoing encroachment of their basic rights. Their account of the steady disregard of their civil liberties includes Dr. Nichols' inability to get one of his patients past an Hassidic/NYPD barricade, and Dr. Nichols' inability to commandeer emergency assistance from the taxpayer-paid ambulance that, like the patrol car, also sits in front of the central Lubavitcher synagogue, seven days a week, 24 hours a day. It is hardly probable that a sixteen-year-old boy, by himself, after midnight, would walk into such an armed, bristling, vigilante-patrolled encampment, let alone accost a young, or an old, or a middle-aged Hassidim! According to eyewitnesses to the beating, Victor was chased by no less than thirty Hassidic men and women on foot, bicycles, in cars and in vans, and finally caught. When Black bystanders tried to stop the beating, they were threatened with guns and told, "Don't come near him, don't touch him."

If there is any truth to Rosenfeld's version that there *was* an Hassidic wedding the night of June 16, this may be what happened: The ceremony took place in the large Hassidic center on the north side of Eastern Parkway. At the conclusion of same, there would have been an outpouring of Hassidim, back and forth across Eastern Parkway, between the Center and the Synagogue. Therefore, Victor, returning to his party, would have been forced to pass through a general milling crowd of Hassidim, no matter which side of the Parkway he elected to travel. Since it was Saturday, approximately 12:25 A.M., and the Hassidic Sabbath, both northern and southern service roads of Eastern Parkway between Brooklyn and Kingston avenues would have been blocked by NYPD/Hassidic barricades. If Victor attempted to pass through, one of the Yeshiva students may have noticed this stranger and, angered at this "intrusion," called out to him. Victor, vastly outnumbered, and surrounded, must have begun to run at that point, trying to reach safety, in the direction of Union Street, a few blocks west. Hassidim on foot, on bicycles, in cars and vans, hastily joined in a mob chasing of the youth. They caught up with him two doors away from "home-free," the Union Street location of the party and his friends. As they fell upon him, according to one Black eyewitness, "It was like the Gestapo."

Further embitterment derives from the common view shared with me by Dr. Nichols, that the Hassidim evade rightful real-estate taxation and that they pursue such bizarre, illegal games as deriving the electricity for the light and the heat of their buildings directly from city street lamps.

At the police precinct for Crown Heights, the 71st, Police Officer John Murdaugh recalled his first confrontation with the Hassidim at "770": A call came through: an ambulance was blocked by the Hassidim and could not get through. Murdaugh and his partner on duty drove to "770," but could accomplish nothing; he called for assistance and cars arrived from four additional precincts, as well: "Cops were knocked to the ground, ribs cracked. And no arrests were made. Personally, I grabbed a couple of prisoners by the wrists and they (other Hassidim) pulled the prisoners away. Somebody tried to steal my gun out of my holster." How could there be no arrests? Murdaugh shrugged and, as he said, later that evening on WPIX-TV, "They (the Hassidim) control the 71st." Murdaugh cites numerous episodes illustrating the hatred the Hassidim bear toward the Black majority around them. For example, as the recording officer on duty, he has been denied entrance to the office/dwellingplace of Hassidic complainants who declared, "No schwartze! No schwartze!"

When I queried Officer Murdaugh about his initial reaction to the assault upon Victor Rhodes, he made this response, without hesitation: "They did it again; this is the most severe incident, but it happened before when the Hassidim go on outbreaks of 'protecting themselves,' as they call it: an overkill." And how does he feel about it? "I am very much uptight because in a couple of years from now my son will be fifteen and it could happen to him. Or my brother might be passing through the precinct. Or—" Murdaugh hesitated, and his voice lowered, slightly—"it might've been me."

Meanwhile, New York City's Police Commissioner refused to transfer or suspend the policemen implicated in the murder of Arthur Miller. He denied that "excessive force" had been employed in the "incident." And the city's Mayor Koch appointed an emergency committee (not one member from Central Brooklyn) and sent his Deputy Mayor, Herman Badillo, on a mission to "cool," to "defuse" the crisis. Presumably pursuant to these goals, Badillo met with spokesmen of the Hassidic community, among them Rabbi Rosenfeld.

"The idiocy" and "the utter insensitivity" of such political decisions, in the words of Reverend Daughtry, stand revealed, and glaring, if one considers that "cooling out" and "defusing" a situation are not identical to a quest for justice. And, if one recalls that it is not a son of the Lubavitcher Hassidim who lies beaten into a coma, but rather a child of Black people, then Black evaluation of the Mayor's conduct as blatantly contemptuous can be understood. Rather than consult with leaders of the aggrieved community, the Mayor's deputy met with representatives of the acknowledged perpetrators of the crime.

"... I will fear no evil."

Whatever the reasons for the steady national rollback on programs of Black enablement, and whatever the reasons for the escalating outbreaks of white violence against Black lives, the tacticians, if there were any, have made an enormous mistake. I believe that the meaning of Crown Heights is this: that we, First World peoples in these United States, have been hurtled against a wall of such brutal and disrespectful resistance to our needs—"Nay, our God-given rights," as Rev. Daughtry has said, so eloquently—that we will be silent, we will be afraid, no more. In this sense, "the seventies" of hidden, whispering misery are over, from Brooklyn to Detroit to Oakland, to the prison cell where they murdered Stephen Biko. Issues intrinsic to Crown Heights, the issue of separation of powers between the church/synagogue and the state; the issue of (police) force uncontrolled by respect for the lives it nevertheless presumes to govern; the issue of the few and the many, and of privilege juxtaposed to impotence enforced by institutional hatred; the issue of power versus the values of justice: these are not issues peculiar to Brooklyn, or even to America, in its entirety.

Hence, it seems useful to bear witness to the turning around, to the resurrection of the spirit, that I have been seen and felt and heard in Black Brooklyn, since the night of the hospitalization of Victor Rhodes.

In Rev. Daughtry's House of the Lord's Church, I have seen my people rise, shouting as one, to the call for intensive voter registration, which Daughtry deems essential to the surcease of Black "powerlessness."

At Unity Night Rally, I have seen Nationalist Black leader Ji-Tu Weusi and the Black candidate for the 14th Congressional District, Dr. Bernard Gifford (formerly Deputy Chancellor of the Board of Education) and New York State Senator Vander Beatty, and on and on, actually set aside their differences, and resolve to act as one to obtain rightful and appropriate political representation of Black people.

At a meeting called to create a Black safety patrol of Crown Heights, in that packed auditorium, I had to abandon my efforts to count up the youths, the different kinds of Black men of all persuasions, resolved that, as Frederick Douglass remarked, "he who is whipped easiest is whipped oftenest" and that, therefore, we will no longer allow our children, our women, and our men to be victims available to those who despise our presence even on earth.

And I heard the Reverend Clarence Norman declare that, the previous night, some 500 Crown Heights middle-class homeowners had convened in one place where they endorsed the patrol and where they joined with the NAACP in calling for a federal investigation of the terrible violence inflicted upon Black life in their community, and a federal investigation of the Lubavitcher Hassidim. As Reverend Heron Sam, of St. Mark's Episcopal Church in Crown Heights, declared: "I want to go after the same funds that the Hassidim have and are using to break the law!"

160

And I watched former Police Sergeant William Hargrave, formerly of the 77th Precinct, face down the hissing and the boos that broke, spontaneously, from among the several hundreds gathered in that one room, and I heard him wait out that reception so that he could say quietly into the mike: "I was a Black man when I joined the Police Department; I'm a Black man tonight," and then proceed to offer his expertise to the formulating patrol. And it was no longer rhetoric, nor hope, but actual history developing, real, in front of my eyes. And I saw and felt the blinding tears of the instantaneous, standing ovation accorded to the mother of Victor Rhodes as she expressed her wish that she could join in protecting our children as she wished she could have protected her own son, and as she voiced her gratitude, even as she trembled, saying, "I call them Modern Day Hitlers, to have done such a thing. And I give thanks to know that we will have justice and not more murder . . ."

And there was Reverend Daughtry, indefatigable, and surely the spiritual, charismatic center of this history, almost inaudible as he stepped forward to reassure Mrs. Rhodes that he, that all of us, would not rest until justice was won.

And afterward I could hear Mr. Oauattara of the O.A.U. avow the certainty of increasing Black African support for the cause of Black Americans and, as I went out into the shadow of the valley of death, that evening, for the first time in several days, I felt safe. And I gave thanks in my heart because this safety rested on the rock of so many of us ashamed and aroused into effective unity, at last: *my cup overfloweth:* and I heard in my head the words of Mrs. Alice Stokes, mother of six and eyewitness to the incredible attack upon Victor Rhodes, heard her telling me to tell mothers throughout these United States, "You need to stress love for one another. No matter what race. That would help, I think." *Surely goodness and mercy:* and I heard the words of Victor's legal guardian, Mr. Maeso McCrae, saying, "I might forgive but I don't never forget; I want justice, I want justice. That's what I want: justice!" And I saw again, Mr. McCrae begin to weep, as he looked at the photo of Victor that I held out to him, while he bit into his underlip and said, "That's him! That's him!" *all the days of my life:* And I flashed back to Victor's younger brother surrounded by his friends on the hood of a car, the hurt all over his soft features, and I fastened upon another eyewitness to Victor's near death: sixteen-year-old Dee Snyder, and his running buddies, standing as tall, shoulders as squared away, as possible, on the spot where it happened, and looking the camera into its eye. Dee told me: "These white people, they really want to hurt you if they catch you, so," he says, gesturing to his sidekicks, "we always travel in a little band of three or four." It was broad daylight and the horrors of Crown Heights wavered in and out of focus in the heat but I grew steady, looking at these children trying to be men before I took the picture of them, right there where it happened: *And I will fear no evil:* "Take care of yourself," we yelled to each other, the kids and I. And that was what we meant, exactly.

20 Black History as Myth (1979)

In 1979, the *New York Times Book Review* published my review of Michele Wallace's book *Black Macho and the Myth of the Superwoman*, under the title *To Be Black and Female*.

At the time, I was working in collaboration with two other Black women artists, Bernice Reagon and Ntozake Shange, on a performance to be held at the Public Theatre. We called our evening of music, song, and poetry *In the Spirit of Sojourner Truth*. This was the very kind of thing that *Black Macho* declared was nonexistent. Zaki and Bernice and I came together because we trusted each other's strength and because we knew we could skip the idiocy of competition for the sake of a political and artistic goal: the raising of an absolutely contemporaneous tribute to the spirit of Sojourner Truth. The outcome of our collaboration, that evening at the Public Theatre, remains one of those moments in my life that irreversibly changed everything from there, because it gave me imperturbable reasons for faith.

At the end of the 1960s, American mass media rolled the cameras away from Black life and the quantity of print on the subject became too small to read. As a result, the number of books published by and about Black people has been negligible since the beginning of this decade. For this reason alone, Michele

Wallace's *Black Macho and the Myth of the Superwoman* is ready-made for commercial exploitation. Its destiny, so far, has been further assured by nearly unprecedented promotion and publicity.

Before the book's publication, *Ms.* magazine departed from its routine policies and published its January 1979 issue under a cover featuring a close-up photograph of a Black woman's face—the face of Michele Wallace. It was accompanied by an announcement: "the book that will shape the 1980s." Shortly afterward, her publisher mailed out a four-color fold-up heralding Miss Wallace's book as one that "could change history." These were claims of singular portent.

You might well imagine that anything so described must serve some urgent purpose. But whatever the motives behind this media launching of the book, they nowhere seem to mesh with the urgency that underlies today's renewed political coming together of Black men and women.

Black Macho and the Myth of the Superwoman is divided into two rather short, somewhat repetitive essays. In the first, Miss Wallace subjects the "Civil Rights Movement" and the "Black Power Movement" to a sexual analysis of Black male and female relations. She asserts that male chauvinism on the part of Black leadership led to the disaffection of Black women and a consequent "end" of the movements. She asserts that Black male preoccupation with white concepts of manhood de-emphasized "patriarchal" priorities such as responsibility for family, engendered adolescent macho posturings such as the riots of Watts and Detroit, and led to Black Panther-style confrontations with white power. For Black men, Miss Wallace says, sex with white women was proof of their freedom.

About Black leadership, she writes, "One could say, in fact, that the Black man risked everything—all the traditional goals of revolution: money, security, the overthrow of the government—in the pursuit of the immediate sense of his own power." And, "The Black revolutionary of the sixties calls to mind nothing so much as a child who is acting for the simple pleasure of the reaction he will elicit from, the pain he will cause, his father." And: "It is interesting to note how various male leaders are recouping in the aftermath of their abominable failure to effect any changes in the lives of the masses of Black people." Alternating with such fierce and freehand generalities are other pronouncements that reveal an astounding ignorance at best: "The most highly organized group the movement had to offer was the Black Muslims." (Note: The Muslims are the one group that made a special point of not being a part of any movement that was preeminently activist or that advocated confrontational strategy vis-à-vis white violence and privilege.) Or: "Like Martin Luther King, Baldwin was an anachronism come the sixties." (Note: If true, this last would mean that the eight years preceding the 1968 assassination of Dr. King bespoke no more than a seismic and national habit of hallucination.)

Here is Miss Wallace on the function of white women for the Black leader of the sixties: "As his Americanization became more and more total, he was conditioned to define his rebellion in terms of the white nightmare. He accepted as appropriate the white man's emphasis on his sexuality ... the notion of the Black man's access to white women as a prerequisite of his freedom was reinforced."

At one point Michele Wallace refers to movement struggles from 1963 through 1965 in this way: "It wasn't the spectacle of the evening news so much as the appearance of a strangely related phenomenon that, more than anything else, made us aware that a new day was coming. Black boys at New Lincoln [her private school] started dating white girls." Her peculiar revisions of history are further marred by such obvious errors as giving 1968 as the date when the Student Nonviolent Coordinating Committee became nationalistic, though its Black position paper was actually issued in 1966. Throughout, her arguments rest on glittering declarations like this one: "But the contemporary Black man no longer exists for his people or even for himself."

In the second essay, Miss Wallace writes, "I think that the Black woman thinks of her history and her condition as a wound which makes her different and therefore special and therefore exempt from human responsibility." Presumably such a hateful perspective explains her mention of Ruby Doris Smith Robinson as merely "a powerful Black woman in S.N.C.C." when, in fact, she was elected executive director in 1966; it may also explain her arrogant derision of Angela Davis as a "Do-it-for-your-man" non-heroine of those times or her reference to Harriet Tubman and Sojourner Truth as women "whom no man in his right mind would want except, perhaps, patient Old Uncle Tom" or her allusion to Fannie Lou Hamer as simply someone who had "spunk."

En route to that assessment of Black women, she offers her theory about "the superwoman," to wit: We (Black women) have internalized myths that depict us as incredibly resilient/strong/aggressive, and possessing social and economic advantages over Black men. Consequently, the resentment Black men bear toward us because they, too, accept these myths, seems to us partly justified, and we, in response to our own guilt, defer to Black men, abdicate our own fulfillment and possible contributions to our people. Whatever its merits, this is hardly a new idea.

Back in 1968, Frances M. Beale, a Black woman and a member of S.N.C.C., composed an essay dealing with hurtful aspects of Black male and female interrelations. "Double Jeopardy: To Be Black and Female" emphasized three points: that Black Women would not "exchange a white master for a Black master," that "the ideology of male supremacy was divisive and backward and had no place in the Black Movement" and that "having babies for the revolution" and "walking three steps behind your man" were concepts counter-productive to the rightful struggle of Black people. Frances Beale presented this document at a S.N.C.C. staff meeting (mainly Black males) in 1968, and it was then adopted as the official S.N.C.C. position on women. The paper was subsequently published in various anthologies and in a 1975 issue of *Black Scholar* that was devoted altogether to Black women.

In any event, it is not easy to follow the "superwoman" argument because Miss Wallace dots her essay with frivolous and distorted observations: She remembers having, in her own childhood, "only an establishment of poverty and oppression thinly veiled by a few trips to Europe, a private school education, and some clothes from Bonwit Teller"; elsewhere she writes that the fury of Black people against whites is "water under the bridge"; then, "As we can see . . . there was some low-key directionless complaining and grumbling among Black women in the sixties. But they put more energy into their fight against women's liberation than into anything else." Later, talking about unmarried Black women who have children, she says, "It certainly can't be for love of children." And, in conclusion to all of this, she writes: "The Black woman never really dealt with the primary issues of the Black movement. . . . She forced herself to be submissive and passive . . . But then, suddenly, the Black movement was over. Now she has begun to straighten her hair again . . . to rouge her cheeks furiously . . . She has little contact with other Black women, and if she does, it is not of a deep sort."

You do have to concede champion qualities to Miss Wallace's capacity for the unsubstantiated, self-demeaning, ahistorical pronouncement. And from her total account of things, it is really hard to tell who is supposed to be more contemptible: the Black man or the Black woman. Nor can I even guess what she is *for:* what she loves, what she respects.

The author was twelve years old in 1964. Obviously, then, none of the pivotal generalizations about the 1960s derives from her own experience. From where, then? Don't ask me: there is not a direct quotation from an interview that she conducted with a living Black man or woman in the entire book. Her conclusions make clear that such people as she may have queried were only strangely related to the cataclysmic, nation-convulsing events that she presumes to analyze. How else can you explain her staggering reduction of the Civil Rights Movement, of Black Nationalism, to an "issue" of interracial dating.

I mean, a whole lot of people died. And everybody who was there—Black women, Black men, and white men and white women—all of the freedom fighters who came together to create an irreversible, revolutionary moment, all risked their lives. It was *not* casual.

A similar need for collective affirmation, for political resistance, by Black people is no less important today than it was when Birmingham became an international name for horror:

The Bakke decision, Proposition 13, Sears, Roebuck's lawsuit against Equal Employment Opportunity programs, the Weber vs. Kaiser Aluminum case pending in the Supreme Court—these are a few clues to a swift and radical reversion to national policies of systematic exclusion and disablement of Black life.

Then how does it happen that the book I have been reading, the book "that could change history," is nothing more nor less than a divisive, fractious tract devoid of hope and dream, devoid even of a competent scholarship that would signify respect for the subject so glibly undertaken?

Why did Michele Wallace write this book? And, I wonder, how does it happen that this book has been published—this book and not another that would summarily describe Black people to ourselves, and to the other ones who watch us so uneasily.

It is something to think about, indeed.

21 Beyond Apocalypse Now (1980)

My host, Michael Ford, kindly let me know that partly in response to this speech Lewis and Clark was going to join with nine other Oregon universities to begin a Visiting Minorities Program throughout the state.

Altogether I spent the first three months of 1980 on the road: out by myself in an America I had never imagined, an America that probably had never even thought about me, about a Black woman poet carrying her song into any house that let her inside. What was she doing here? In Minnesota, in Oregon, in California, in Kentucky?

That was what I wondered, myself, through the many nights alone in the hotel of another strange town. But the feedback Michael Ford gave me in Oregon, and the face-to-face reactions that people expressed wherever I read my poetry gave me the benefit of a reality check, and more: It seemed that the trip was not a waste and this country not a wasteland and the people were not, everywhere, my enemies. One afternoon, I think it was in Lexington, Kentucky, a young Black girl came up to me, after a rap session on Black poetry. "Where is your home?" she asked me in her soft, southern voice. I thought about it and then I said, "I'm home."

Stepping into the penultimate ten years of the century, I find myself in St. Paul, Minnesota: Heartland/Breadbasket/Midwest America. It's almost the end of January. It's 45 degrees below zero.

Every conceivable walkway lies under an undulant surface of ice up to three inches thick. Seldom does the pedestrian find even a foot of concrete safely exposed or the ice tempered by salt or sand. Apparently, the idea is Don't Walk. Drive—even from your front door down to your car at the curb.

Besides the omnipresent ice, I realize how far away from home I am because, although houses hereabouts boast a solid interior warmth that Nordic practices of construction and that first quality storm windows guarantee, from a living room couch I listen to occasional cars outside as they slide, zigzag, through the icebound avenues. Count them: one car in two minutes, then no car, possibly, for another minute. These mere tracings of traffic sounds testify to the otherwise ordinary silence of the place. It's bare. It's very big and very quiet. It's clean. In three weeks I have not seen a garbage can, nor any littering.

Nor have I seen, since reaching St. Paul, high-rise apartment housing; instead, the evidently usual lifestyle insists upon a fully detached single family house complete with the indicative red brick chimney breaking through the roof.

Nor have I seen folks generally attempting to walk around and, when I do spot another more or less upright traveler, it is either an isolate being or it is a conventional and heterosexual couple married in fact and/or by contractual agreement. In three weeks I have seen extremely few instances of two or three adults who are simply friends going somewhere or who have arrived, somewhere, together. There are no guys standing on any corner. Always it's the comparatively exclusive couple or else it's the lone agent hobbling, driving, or jogging through the cold, in sneakers that mostly resemble steel-belted radial tires.

It's white. Ten days after my arrival here I thought I saw a Black man leaving a dry cleaner's, nearby; after I mentally doublechecked that impression and concluded that he really was a Black man, and by the time I doubled back in his direction, he was gone. He had vanished. And, with his disappearance, only I remained, moving bulky, small, and dark among the polar winds.

You could say that Minnesota represents the heart of whiteness for this visitor, this Black woman who grew up inside the center city neighborhood of Bedford-Stuyvesant, in Brooklyn. You could say that, for me, 45 degrees below zero plus blizzard snows blowing about my face and my feet, you could say that the melodramatic severity of this place signifies apocalypse, right now.

What should I do? You think I should organize a search-and-destroy series of missions out on the slippery streets? You think I should colonize every available Scandinavian and conscript him or her into carrying my groceries as well as my other, personal supplies? You think I should steal as many ski sweaters and down jackets as I can find and then ship them the hell out of here, maybe ship them back to Brooklyn? You think I should drill through the ice, for oil? You think I should let myself go bananas and then blame it on the snow? You think I could get away with a claim of Overwhelming Evil Environment that will excuse me if I kill a score or two of whitefolks? What should I do?

I know I should do *something*. All of Western tradition, from the late bloom of the British Empire right through the early doom of Vietnam dictates that *you do something spectacular and irreversible* whenever you find yourself in or whenever you impose yourself upon a wholly unfamiliar situation belonging to somebody else. Frequently it's your soul or your honor or your manhood, or democracy itself, at stake.

As I write these words on a Sunday evening here, in Minnesota, I am somewhat at a loss. I am not sure just which supremely valuable part of my identity needs defense against these unfamiliar and, therefore, presumably vile environs. True, it's extremely cold outside. You could lose your fingertips or toes or an ear, I suppose. But me? I'm inside a house much like the houses that the natives regularly choose for shelter; so I'm okay, I think.

But since I am the Visiting Black Poet at a 99.6 percent white college perhaps my name/my racial identity is in danger. Perhaps I should refuse to learn the name of any of the natives and, instead, efficiently refer to students and faculty, alike, as aborigines or as *bitch* or *son of a bitch*, depending. On the weekends, perhaps I should firebomb the ski slopes or scorch the slumbering wheat fields into cinderland. And rather than peering through eyelash dazzlement as the softly falling snow melts into my eyes, perhaps I should more correctly perceive the snow as yet another insidious level of subversion by Abominable Atmosphere. Oh, what should I do?

It sure is hard for me to follow in the footsteps of white men!

Apocalypse Now, one of those multimultimillion-dollar brainstorms, came to the screen well advertised as "the definitive film about Vietnam." Remembering how Vietnam, that victim country and its victorious people, remembering how that American war, with its long-term American atrocities, shook apart America and forever tore down the previous distinctions, in my mind, between *racism* and *imperialism*, I wanted to see this celluloid extravaganza. I went. To my amazement, *Apocalypse Now* fairly well abandons Vietnam, the War in Vietnam, after the first thirty minutes. At no time during this "definitive treatment of Vietnam" do you learn the name of a single Vietnamese human being, nor is there so much as a lame attempt to show the regular days and nights of Vietnamese people, nor to document the prolonged American military ravishment of that orderly and peaceable existence. Instead you confront American atrocities presented in a consistently flashy style so that you cannot surmount purely technical dimensions such as the skill of the cinematographer or the explosive power of a particular kind of bomb.

After the first thirty minutes, the film settles closely upon the question of the ill- or well-being of two white men: one white man searching for the other one who presides over a bizarre little kingdom at the end of a hinterland river. Images blur wildly into projections simply of the inner consciousness of the journeying white man on his way to meet the other one. At the film's climax, the viewer beholds a multiplicity of horrendous evidence: the finally found, the other white man, is a homicidal maniac, at least. He has rewarded the appalling deference and loyalty of the natives with altogether unrequited butchery.

On the way to this climax, there is a scene when a peasant

boat is stopped and the civilian (excuse me, the *native*) passengers are slaughtered by American soldiers. Besides myself, many other people in the theater audience gagged aloud at that episode. One of two white men seated behind me called out, "So? They do it to us!" "Yeah?" I answered, "Where? Where?" I gather those particular white men did not understand the point I was making since they continued to whisper, "What did she say? What?" And that moment I was too angry to bother to clarify what seemed so obvious to me: Third World peoples have *never*, in all of world history, landed armies on a white man's territory such as Rome, Brussels, London, or St. Paul, and then proceeded to annihilate whomever and whatever they discovered in that alien place. I mean, Vietnam does not belong to America. Never did.

The notion that you can invade the country of another people, kill them, mine the waters, burn the earth, and then claim equal rights of self-defense if and when the indigenous survivors retaliate derives from a mentality so hideous, so self-absorbed, as to stagger my mind, completely.

But the film, *Apocalypse Now*, develops this perspective even further. Through nauseating slow closeups we wallow in the wisdom acquired by the murderer, the white man, found at the end of the terrible river. We are told that in this unfamiliar place, this jungle, this remote countryside of an alien people you will finally realize just how many things exist beyond judgments of good or evil. There is, in fact, only "the horror, the horror." In other words, the butcher exculpates himself, entirely, through ponderous mouthings of bathos presented as heavy-duty retrospect and revelation.

The premise of this story pivots upon an evaluation of every non-European as a creature who must be, therefore, "a primitive savage" living in an un-American, a non-European climate and circumstance that is "barbarous" and "evil" because it is unfamiliar to the European or American intruder. Said European will collapse, there, into a nigger version, as it were, of his true, more virtuous, and lighter/whiter self. Hence it is never the white colonialist who is the savage or the barbarian. Rather it is the savage and/or the barbaric *surroundings* of the white man that will compel his untoward display of a nigger identity: i.e., an acting out of his "dark" emotions/his "dark" thoughts, et cetera. Extraordinary.

"The horror" this film means you to grasp is not what America has done to the Vietnamese but rather what Vietnam has done to two white men! Heat, isolation, unfamiliarity with the look of a people and a place—these must be gruesome hardships, indeed, for the fruit of America's manhood.

Underlying *Apocalypse Now* is the novella by Joseph Conrad, *Heart of Darkness*, which has been riveted into the core curriculum of every liberal arts college in the United States. Given its continuous life as a prime element of American socialization, I have thought to reread that de facto classic of Western literature.

In Conrad's version it is the Congo and not Vietnam. We center upon two white men in that quote dark unquote continent. Now I have always despised this story as a preeminent contrivance of racist mythology. But this recent reading has deepened my disgust. It would seem that latterday/enlightened critics of Conrad perceive him as a "melancholy" but nevertheless sensitive moralist aghast at the practices of colonialism, of imperialism.

Again and again they remind you that Conrad once described his witness to Belgian colonialism as "the distasteful knowledge of the vilest scramble for loot that ever disfigured the history of human conscience and geographical exploration." What a hero, right? At the beginning of *Heart of Darkness* you furthermore meet with this sentiment as it spews forth from the narrator, Marlow's, mouth: "The conquest of the earth, which mostly means the taking it away from those who have a different complexion or slightly flatter noses than ourselves, is not a pretty thing when you look into it too much." But, Conrad continues, "What redeems it is the idea only." Theft, murder, rape, and all the ancillary acts of colonialism have been "redeemed," in one sentence, by an idea? What could that idea be?

It is nothing more than the concept of "civilizing the savages" or, in other words, the aim of changing these different, these innocent peoples into facsimiles of himself, his own evil.

174

At the very best, this *unthink* describes a practically miraculous magnitude of self-deceit and delusion.

And how does it happen that whenever a white man wishes to encounter the evil of his own soul he must position that truth outside his natural clime, customs, relationships, and, instead, immerse himself in "darkness": i.e., among Third World peoples/peoples less powerful than he/peoples innocently prey to his performance of one or another monstrous crime for the sake of a solipsistic exploration?

Let me cite two entries from Conrad's *Congo Diaries* of 1890:

"Friday, 4th July . . . saw another dead body lying by the path in an attitude of meditative repose . . . At night when the moon rose heard shouts and drumming in distant villages. Passed a bad night."

"Saturday, 5th July . . . Today fell into a muddy puddle— Beastly! The fault of the man that carried me. After camping went to a small stream bathed and washed clothes. Getting jolly sick of this fun."

If you ever wished for a two-liner depicting the colonial white attitude toward every so-called heart of darkness be it Vietnam, the Congo, or Manhattan, there it is: *"Today fell into a muddy puddle—Beastly! The fault of the man that carried me."*

Notice that the fact of a dead African on the path the day before does not elicit a comparable response from melancholy Joseph Conrad: *That* is not "beastly." What is the death of a Black man compared to the momentary fall of a white man into a mud puddle? Obviously, not much. You can read *Heart of Darkness* until you lose the capacity to see and you will know nothing about the real, particular lives of the African peoples Conrad trespassed among. It is the same as the movie it spawned: *Apocalypse Now.*

A couple days after seeing that film I had urgent reason to resign from the national, white, and supposedly feminist publication *Chrysalis*. As I explained in my letter of resignation, I took this action to protest their consistently racist editorial policies whereby the priorities and the distinctive perspectives of Black and Third World women never break into print. Within a few weeks I found myself the recipient of a barrage of Xeroxed copies of letters written from one white woman to another. Rather than acknowledge my criticisms/my resignation, rather than address the specific political Third World concerns I raised, these well-known white feminists used the occasion as an opportunity to re-examine personal relationships between them: between one white woman and some other white woman. Once again, this was a pretty bad movie about the souls of white-folks who seek to discover themselves by annihilating me.

This episode in what some women like to describe as feminist herstory-making fits perfectly into the allegedly patriarchal model of *Heart of Darkness*. It lets me conclude one pseudo-quandary created by mass media since the sixties: "What's been more determining for you, the fact that you're Black or the fact that you're female?" Colonial mentality, colonial self-absorption is not limited to men: never has been. And more often than not it is the darkness of my skin and not my gender that seems to precipitate holocaust invasions of my life, whether you look at things on the scale of a Black community or on the scale of the entire African continent.

At any rate, here I am. I'm not going anywhere. As a matter of fact, despite evaluations of the United Nations as "a zoo" and despite popular characterizations of Third World leaders as "cannibals" we, the stubborn majority of this world, are not about to disappear.

I sit inside this St. Paul, Minnesota, living room, nervously aware of my position: a Black poet in the Heart of White America. What should I do?

I suppose I could run out and kill somebody, some savage passer-by, just to show I'm only human and rather far away from home. But instead tonight I choose to look back upon the seventies. I name to myself those nation states and their peoples who seek to achieve actual political sovereignty: Vietnam, Chile, the People's Republic of Angola, the inextinguishable Palestinian concept of Palestine, Nicaragua, Iran. And I think I should sit easy, for a minute, and be very happy. Long ago, in my lifetime, the only miracle was Cuba, against the U.S.A. Now check out the map!

In the traditional white concept of the *Heart of Darkness*,

Marlow goes looking for ivory and Kurtz, but meanwhile, the Belgian Congo no longer exists. The savages have tired of colonial ravagings through their woods and waterways. The two white men, Marlow and Kurtz, take up jogging—separately, of course—and one of them stops smoking and the other becomes a vegetarian and both of them, separately, pursue continuing adult education courses and one of them joins a creative writing workshop and both of them meditate, separately, and each of them sees a therapist twice a week, and meanwhile the hungry and the illiterate and the despised peoples of the world gather themselves into a functional, a collective identity that means an irreversible destruction of the privileges of violence.

In this heart of whiteness where I see separate runners and separate couples and separate houses and one person in a car that seats five and ice and so much snow and ice and where I shake from the cold air stinging me to tears and where I brace myself to manage so much ice so much subzero inhospitality to the concept, even, of a warm and beating human heart, the heart of the social animals we have been rumored to be, what should I do?

And if I join the self-absorption the self-improvement the self-discovery the jogging of the natives who surround me what will we do when all of us stop running? Will we arrive anywhere, together?

Is there, in fact, somebody else alive, besides each one of us?

Is there some way to prove that there is somebody else alive, without violence?

I would suppose that these questions will yield a radical plan for all the rest of my life. And yours.

22 Civil Wars (1980)

Sometimes it is sitting in the middle of a room with 200 other people. The name of the meeting or committee doesn't matter. You light a cigarette. That doesn't help. You take notes or raise your hand. That doesn't help. The problem is not a procedural point of order or the particular identity of the leader. Everybody's on best behavior: politely taking turns, preparing to vote or write letters. The problem is the yearning courtesies, the underlying patience, the honcho upfront and the followers who face him, or her.

Most likely the reason people came together was because something wrong, something rather extraordinary fell into their lives. Everybody in the room has been smashed by the same ax, and look at the gathering. Look at the meaning of the manners of the scene!

It reminds me of instant TV coverage when there's a disaster: A baby has been burned to death. The TV reporter approaches the surviving parents as they stand, dumfounded by horror, on the street.

"How do you feel about the loss of your little girl?" the reporter asks, moving the microphone close to the mouth of the father. The young man, confronted by a microphone and cameras, struggles to recall what etiquette requires of him.

"Well," he manages to reply. "Of course we're in a state of shock. (Pause.) This is a terrible night in our lives. (Pause.)"

But the reporter does not remove the microphone. Instead, there's a second question.

"What will you and your wife do now?"

The young man puts his arm around his wife and says, politely, "I don't know. We don't know."

In the context of tragedy, all polite behavior is a form of self-denial. I can remember being eight years old and there was my mother warning me to watch *the tone of my voice* in the middle of a violent fight between my father and myself. The purpose of polite behavior is never virtuous. Deceit, surrender, and concealment: these are not virtues. The goal of the mannerly is comfort, per se. I can remember my father leaving me alone, finally, when there was no longer space for consideration of my tone: When I pulled a knife from under my pillow and asked him, "What do you want?" it was then that he changed his mind: What he wanted, then, was somebody else to beat up.

Nevertheless, people lose their jobs or their lives and still the reaction is cooperative. We try to speak clearly and to spare the feelings of the listener. We shave and shower and put on a clean shirt for the meeting. We volunteer to make phone calls, or coffee, or submit to the outcome of a vote about what shall I do. I have been raped: Who will speak for me? What are the bylaws?

The courtesies of order, of ruly forms pursued from a heart of rage or terror or grief defame the truth of every human crisis. And that, indeed, is the plan: To defuse and to deform the motivating truth of critical human response to pain.

In his essay "The Pleasures of Hating," William Hazlitt earned himself the reputation of an irascible, outrageous crank by passionate lament for earlier and multiple occasions when he had permitted himself only a diluted/inadequate expression of his anger and hurt and thorough disgust. In my teens, I was shocked, awake, by that panegyric to the forbidden emotion. And I was haunted by the devious, the plaintive love so clearly protected by his reverence for the truth of things, especially the hateful truth of things.

But the lobby for polite behavior is fairly inescapable. Most often, the people who can least afford to further efface and deny the truth of what they experience, the people whose very existence is most endangered and, therefore, most in need of vigilantly truthful affirmation, these are the people—the poor and the children—who are punished most severely for departures from the civilities that grease oppression.

If you make and keep my life horrible then, when I can tell the truth, it will be a horrible truth; it will not sound good or look good or, God willing, feel good to you, either. There is nothing good about the evils of a life forced into useless and impotent drift and privation. There is very little that is attractive or soothing about being strangled to death, whether it is the literal death of the body or the actual death of the soul that lying, that the humiliation and the evil of self-denial, guarantees.

Extremity demands, and justifies, extreme response. Violation invites, and teaches, violence. Less than that, less than a scream or a fist, less than the absolute cessation of normal events in the lock of abnormal duress is a lie and, worse than that, it is blasphemous ridicule of the self.

Nonetheless, I am a liar. I am frequently polite. I go to meetings and sit, properly, in one chair. I write letters to Washington. It's been a long while since I actually hit anybody at all.

One of my friends is Frances Fox Piven. We became friends by fighting each other in the realm of tactics, during the early sixties. Frances was advocating rehabilitation of the ghetto. I was advocating that she, a white intellectual, mind her own damn business. And I was advocating a push for integration because I thought that, otherwise, you might achieve better housing for Black families but you would still lack supporting community services such as reliable garbage collection, police protection, and ambulance response. We did not change each other's minds but we did come to respect the sincerity of our differences. And then we became close friends.

At this time Frances was living in Harlem with her daughter, Sara, who was just a few years older and a few inches taller than my son, Christopher. Each of us was raising one child and also pursuing a complicated professional and political life.

You could accurately describe Frances as a brilliant and radical humanitarian; her commitment to poor people and to Black people cannot, anywhere, be easily matched.

But there are things that we never talk about, or never talk about, twice. Until a few months ago, as a matter of fact, the silent areas between us led me to let the friendship atrophy, for almost two years.

We'd met for lunch in the Village. She was very angry about my piece in *Seven Days*, the one about the Hassidim and Victor Rhodes. On the street, as we walked to the restaurant, I asked her about the impending referendum in California, the one that would mean, if it passed, that a teacher who expressed the opinion that sexual preference was not the business of the state could then be fired. "Oh, Gay Rights," she said. "No," I said, "Civil Rights."

Well, about this we disagreed, and seriously. Of course, that had been an area of silence between us for many years: "Gay Rights," or my loving a woman, these were subjects excluded from the compass of her radical humanitarian concern. Compared to unemployment or shrunken Welfare moneys or hunger, Frances viewed such "deviant behavior" as frivolous distraction from these other, unarguably gut issues.

At lunch, our argument became a furious exchange. Frances felt that my identification of the Lubavitch Hassidim assailants of Victor Rhodes, and that my emphatic focus upon Victor and the Black community amounted to an act of anti-Semitism.

It would be hard to say which one of us was more outraged.

I remember thinking that the cafe table where we sat was really as large as the whole country and that now we had taken irreconcilable, opposite sides. It was the survival of her people, as we saw it, poised against the survival of my people.

What about all of our discussions and all of our trust and what about the truth, for God's sake? What about that? The truth, Frances retorted, was not merely that one "incident." The truth had to include the entire history of the Jews so that, for instance, a reader could appreciate the background for instinctive expectations of persecution. I said I didn't think we really should get into a comparison of histories; that seemed inherently otiose to me and no amount of arguing would dissuade either of us from the conviction that our people were suffering long and too long.

I said my concern, at the moment, was not the history of

the Jews or an understanding as to why Hassidic Jews might happen to murder a Black child. My concern was that a Black child had been beaten and that he lay, critical and in a coma, even as we sat in that restaurant, and that somebody Hassidic was responsible and that whoever that might be should be duly prosecuted by the law, and that unless somebody insisted on the facts, in mass media print, the odds against such due process were pretty fucking high.

I said that, to my knowledge, the history of Black people in white America was not a factor in regular press coverage of alleged Black crime: That it was ridiculous to expect more generosity of me than I, than my people, had ever received.

When we parted, Frances gave me a copy of *The Last of the Just*, asking me to read it, in a rather somber voice. I took it home and was bitterly dismayed to find that it is a novel tracing the relentlessly vicious and evil persecution of the Jews through several centuries. This did seem to mean that my friend seriously believed me to be an anti-Semite. I was stunned.

We had finally had a fight beyond tactics. It seemed to me that my silence on these issues and my continuing self-denial around the "issue" of my bisexuality was what had kept the friendship alive. Without my collaboration, without my self-censorship, the disagreements between us seemed irreconcilable.

Whether it was about Zionism or Palestine or my own, evidently, inadmissible feelings, I had chosen to keep silent and to politely slide by, or omit, references to these explosive spaces between us. But now that such silence was broken, and after our fight, I felt I had to make a choice I had never expected to make. And so I did. I chose complete silence. I could no longer participate in an exchange requiring acrobatics of self-denial even for the sake of those real and enormous areas of mutual agreement where I respected Frances as my comrade.

And then the good news of Miami burst upon America. It was such good news. A whole lot of silence had ended, at last! Misbegotten courtesies of behavior were put aside. There were no leaders. There was no organization and no spokesman. There was no agenda. There were no meetings, no negotiations. A violated people reacted with violence. An extremity of want, an extremity of neglect, and extremity of racist oppression had been met, at last, with an appropriate, extreme reaction: an outcry and a reaching for vengeance, a wreaking of havoc in return for wrecked lives, a mutilation of passers-by in return for generations mutilated by contempt and by the immutable mutilations of poverty. Miami was completely impolite.

There was no deceit, no surrender, no concealment.

And why should victims cover for their executioners? Why should the victims cooperate and agree to discuss or write letters about what is as blatant and as deadly as Nagasaki, as horrendous as Hiroshima?

But this has been the code, overwhelmingly, for the oppressed: That you keep cool and calm down and explore proper channels and above all, that you remain law-abiding and orderly precisely because it is the order of the day that you will beg and bleed, precisely because it is the power of the law of the terrorist state arrayed against you to force you to beg and bleed without acceptable recourse except for dumb endurance or mute perishing.

And while the terrorist State, the Bureaus of Welfare, of Unemployment and Education, the Police and the State Troopers and the Army immediately mass, respectively, to confuse or mollify or punish and extirpate the always short-lived incivility of the afflicted, who will punish the violent State?

And how else can you successfully act to punish the State (i.e., *the manner of standing* that is the general condition in which you find yourself) except to eliminate the aping of the manners that were devised to secure your own wretched status, and except by acting so that what stands must fall?

Miami is not without precedent. Past confrontations between striking workers and state violence deployed by management have several times risen to those levels of retaliation, for example. But within the history of Black and white confrontations in America, it has seldom if ever occurred before that the violated Black citizens reached beyond internalized rage and beyond self-destructive symbols to the enemy, himself: to his own courtroom beyond the boundaries of the Black community, and to his own white body.

Various press-appointed and self-acclaimed Black leaders hastened to Miami, hoping "to keep the lid on" and "to cool things down." While a few mumbled one or two words about the justice of protest, all were quick to "condemn and deplore" the "violence and the brutality" of the protest. Not one of those leaders deplored "the violence and the brutality" of the obscenely engendering situation in which the Black people of Florida have been barely living. Not one of them condemned that act of State violence that took away the life of Arthur MacDuffie.

In the massive Black peoples' uprising of Miami, 1980, however, there was no tolerance left for airplane leadership—the leaders who get a call from the White House and then free tickets to fly into and out of a revolution. Nobody listened to these models of professional leadership. In fact, the President himself could not utter a complete lie before he was shouted and pelted away.

Miami was a peoples' uprising, and not an organized demonstration. It was extraordinary; an authentic spontaneous combustion resulting from conflict between life and the degradation of life. It was on site. This was not about making Hong Kong or the Philippines safe for democracy. When this house caught on fire, everybody was home.

I waited and watched to see what would happen next. I looked for the emergence of spokesmen. I listened for news of negotiations urgently begun between city hall and the community. I asked around for the name of a group, a committee: some/any formal and comprehensible and orderly "Miami Rights Coalition" stepping forward with a list of logically enumerated demands, and an eloquent defense of these demands.

None of this happened; Miami was news.

It was anarchy in the best sense: it was pure. By the time the very mention of Miami could bring about shudderings and panic throughout America, the explosion of protest was over; it had not been instigated or conceived as a tactic toward 40 more jobs or five cents more an hour. It was an unadulterated, absolute response to the terrors of a merciless oppression. And it was more: It was an ending of self-hatred. The expression of hatred for your enemies is sometimes the only way to end self-hatred. Where there is conflict, conscious termination of self-hatred is the only means to rational possibilities for love. Miami was an act of love: love for Arthur MacDuffie and love for every jeopardized Black life.

When Miami happened, I had been thinking about leadership, per se. Again and again after the assassination of Martin Luther King, Jr., social commentators "deplored" the lack of Black leadership. But I had been thinking, maybe it's a good thing. Certainly, I couldn't see any white leadership around that left me envious. The concept of leadership itself seemed to me dangerous and tired.

How could you consciously commit yourself to the worldwide movement into self-determination, and then turn around and say where is my leader/who is speaking for me?

My immediate, personal reasons for reconsidering the value of leadership had been exacerbated some six months earlier. At the 1979 organized, nonviolent demonstration to protest the police murder of Luis Baez, and during the police riot that followed, my overwhelming sensation was that of suicidal rerun in the suicidal Black tradition of mass nonviolence:

• A multitude of followers faced a stage from which certain leaders presumed to tell us why we were there and what we felt and how we should march together out of the park. ("Peacefully," and "Four abreast, arms linked.")

• The multitude then followed the leaders into the night whereupon the leaders became invisible and inaudible to most of us, marching behind them. Certainly it was not possible to hear or ascertain what, if anything, the leaders had planned for our safety and for our effective, continuing protest. *Perforce*, we were following, blindly.

• When the police attacked, suddenly it was no longer about following the leadership or leadership responsibility: There were no leaders, only more than one thousand unarmed demonstrators, trapped.

A small group of Black artists and writers who had been trapped by the police attack met at my house to brainstorm and to compile an eyewitness account. Between the night of the

Baez demonstration and the night when our account, accompanied by recommendations for community response, was to be presented at an open People's Tribunal, a Black woman, Elizabeth Magnum, was murdered by the Brooklyn police.

At the People's Tribunal, the spokesperson for our group, Alexis DeVeaux, began her presentation. When she reached the section of the statement that addressed the police murder of Elizabeth Magnum, the honcho in charge of the proceedings came to the microphone and attempted to halt her testimony. Alexis was able to complete it, nonetheless, only because the hundred or so community people seated in the audience roared their approval and support.

After Alexis sat down, the honcho came to the mike and harangued the audience: this is not the place for speeches, he said. This is not the place for anything but the people, the community, and for testimony about police violence!

We left the Tribunal, dazed. When our lives lay at risk on the Brooklyn streets, that particular turkey was nowhere in sight. Now he was playing the leader and presuming to choose who are and who are not "the people." He was presuming to decide, furthermore, what the people can and cannot say! It also occurred to me that I could not recall, North or South, an organized demonstration ever called to protest the death of any Black woman, let alone the murder of Elizabeth Magnum.

And so it came to me that I was sick of professional leaders and that I would never again agree to be cannon fodder for a nonviolent demonstration. I resolved that I was unwilling to be killed, unarmed, and physically allergic to meetings, in general.

It came to me that self-determination has to mean that the leader is your individual gut, and heart, and mind or we're talking about power, again, and its rather well-known impurities. Who is really going to care whether you live or die and who is going to know the most intimate motivation for your laughter and your tears is the only person to be trusted to speak for you and to decide what you will or will not do.

The only leadership I can respect is one that enables every man and woman to be his and her own leader: to abandon victim perspective and to faithfully rely upon the truth of the

186

feeling that is his or hers and then to act on that, without apology.

Neither race nor gender provides the final definitions of jeopardy or refuge. The final risk or final safety lies within each one of us attuned to the messy and intricate and unending challenge of self-determination. I believe the ultimate power of all the people rests upon the individual ability to trust and to respect the authority of the truth of whatever it is that each of us feels, each of us means. On what basis should *what* authority exceed the authority of *this* truth?

And what should we fear? No movement, not the Republican, nor the Black nor the women's nor the environmental movement can exist without you and me. Likewise for leaders. And although Nestle's corporation may circumnavigate the globe and fire its factory workers in Massachusetts and subjugate its workers in the Philippines into peonage and poison the babies in Africa, it is not, finally, impregnable. Nestle's and every other multinational corporation, finally, needs that troublesome, maverick component: the people—you and me.

We are not powerless. We are indispensable despite all atrocities of state and corporate policy to the contrary.

At a minimum we have the power to stop cooperating with our enemies. We have the power to stop the courtesies and to let the feelings be real. We have the power not to vote, and not to register for the draft, and not to applaud, and not to attend, and not to buy, and not to pay taxes or rent or utilities At the very least, if we cannot control things we certainly can mess them up.

Arthur MacDuffie died because three cops beat him to death because he went through a red light and he was Black Where is the feeling about that, outside Miami?

Are the cops that murdered him still walking around? Still cops? Still alive?

My son called me from Cambridge, the Sunday of the Miami uprising. I told him some of my ideas. He said, "Have you read Frances' book?" He meant *Poor Peoples' Movements: Why They Succeed, How They Fail*, by Frances Piven and Richard Cloward. No, I hadn't. "Read it," he said. "You have to."

Actually, what I had to do first was to consider the silence between us. And I did. And I decided to let it stand: to let the failures of the friendship stand and to reach out, instead, to Frances in areas of mutual, urgent concern, to engage once again in talk about tactics of struggle.

I read *Poor Peoples' Movements*, sometimes without stopping to sleep. Here it was: Documented historical proof that we are not powerless, that no one is powerless. With meticulous research and the most scrupulous open analysis of four movements—the unemployed workers' movement, the workers' movement of the Depression, the Civil Rights movement, and then the Welfare Rights movement—Frances Piven and Richard Cloward present a working model for protest in America: for effective, peoples' protest movements. Examining the factors of failure and of victory, they arrive at a paradigmatic construct for radical change in this country: change minus the distortions of leaders on a first-name basis with the enemy. You could look at this book and deeply take heart: That more than once those who have the least defenses against the violence of the powerful have dared to defy that power, dared to confront that violence, with their own. And, more than once, those with the most meager resources to resist oppression have won something important, as the result of that confrontation. And in every instance, it has never been *who is the leader* but rather *who are the people*. It has never been *what is the organization* but *what is the crisis.*

I had some questions to discuss with Frances: If the essence of a peoples' movement is its spontaneity, then how can you sustain it?

But I hesitated. I thought again about all the other things that we would not talk about and all the arguments that would persist between us, and my feeling was, "What the hell; friendship is not a tragedy; we can be polite."

And so I called her up, to talk.

June Jordan was born in Harlem and raised in the Bedford-Stuyvesant section of Brooklyn, where she began writing poetry at the age of seven. Now the author of fourteen books, several of them award winners, she travels widely to speak and read her poems. She has written essays and articles for the *New York Times*, the *Village Voice*, the *New Republic*, *Ms.*, and *Essence*. Her poems have appeared in such publications as *Newsday*, *Ms.*, *American Dialog*, *New Black Poetry*, and *Partisan Review*. Awards include a Rockefeller Grant in Creative Writing, the American Library Association Best Book of the Year, the *New York Times* Outstanding Book of the Year, and the Prix de Rome in Environmental Design, and, most recently, an NEA Grant. She has also been a National Book Award finalist.

Her most recent work is a play—*For The Arrow That Flies By Day*.

Made in the USA
Las Vegas, NV
27 November 2020